The Badgers
of Badger Hill

Grimbart Dass, Tasso, Lady Eleanor Grey, Blair Badger

The Badgers of Badger Hill

David Ross

Illustrated by Jaroslav Bradac

THE WOBURN PRESS—LONDON

First published in Great Britain in 1974 by
WOBURN BOOKS LTD.,
67 Great Russell Street,
London WC1B 3BT.

ISBN 0 7130 0127 5

Text set in 14/16 pt. Photon Baskerville, printed by photolithography,
and bound in Great Britain at The Pitman Press, Bath

CONTENTS

The Badgers
of Badger Hill

ON a hot summer day last year the great Bell Harry Tower of Canterbury Cathedral shimmered in a blue sky above the City. In the hot bustle of the streets of shops below, motor cars revved and droned and changed gear and hooted and groaned their way out of the City and along the road by the river Stour. They hummed into the green country where sheep grazed and hops grew high and thick with their bunches of pale green flowers and apples ripened slowly on trees in the long neat rows of the orchards. Some of the cars hummed up narrow roads into the downs, where their occupants switched off almost boiling engines so that they could get out and stretch their legs and admire the view and, perhaps, have a picnic. So the afternoon passed by and the picnickers set off at last down the hill towards their cars again, their faces pink with sandwiches, beer, lemonade and sunshine.

By the time they were at their cars you could hardly hear their voices from the top of Badger Hill in the woods there. A rabbit appeared, and another, feeding and munching among the rough grass unworriedly as the cars moaned off along the road back to Canterbury, for animals know they have nothing to fear from a moving car as long as they keep off the road. Wasps gathered greedily round a spot of jam that had been dropped at a picnic. The rabbits fed through the long end of the afternoon, and were joined as the sun went down by some pheasants who picked among the heath.

As the evening came on and the shadows lengthened, the wood pigeons returned from the cornfields where they had been feeding and coo-cooed noisily among the branches of the fir plantation, squabbling and flapping for places to roost. A breeze sprang up singing through the firs with a chilly music that seemed to quieten the pigeons. It was quiet as the sun slipped behind the downs. The woods were already dark, although there was still blue evening light on the heath and meadows. An owl began to hoot a hunting cry as he flew from the woods. After he had flown off elsewhere a quiet shape slipped among the shadows from the wood and down across the meadows toward the road. It was a fox, hungry and hunting. The woods were very quiet now. Everything had left, it seemed, or gone to sleep. The breeze had dropped again. The night was silent under summer stars.

Suddenly, at the edge of the pitch black woods, at the sandy mouth of a cavernous black burrow, there was movement. There was a face, long black, with silver arrows along its cheeks. With a rustle and a thump this ghostly creature moved up out of the steep burrow as easily as if the ground were flat. The long head waved left and right, smelling the air with great care for several moments. Then it turned back into its burrow and gave a little yicker. It was safe to come out. As it happened for night after night beyond all counting and for years beyond number, the wild ones were coming out into their kingdom. The badgers were there, moving through the mothy dark, before there were men to give names to these lands; for they are England's oldest surviving inhabitants among large animals.

*TWO
TRAVELLERS*

BLAIR Badger had spoken into the tunnel entrance of his home:

"Come; there is no danger."

But his wife and children were not ready. The badger sat down by his front door and scratched himself and stretched, snuffling.

There was still no sign of his family. He called again.

"I say come forth. There is no danger."
While he waited he dug with his nose happily among the grasses and leaves round the doorway, grunting and snuffling.

He thought: "Of course, as usual, they aren't ready. I could wait all night for them. They still wouldn't be ready when the sun comes up."

He looked at the fine moon sailing in the cloudless night sky, and hummed a little. Then he went back to the burrow entrance and said once again:

"In the name of goodness I say come!"

He turned away again, humming rather more loudly to keep his temper. He stamped up the badger path that led from his door into the woods; then he stamped back. Then he went very slowly down the badger path that led from his front door down towards the pasture and the stream, humming very loudly indeed. All of a sudden he stopped humming.

"Ye gods!" he said. "What on earth are they doing down there?"

He galloped at full tilt back up the steep path to his front door, and as he thrust his head into the burrow, he shouted:

"What on earth are you doing down there?"

It so happened that, as he had thrust his head down into the tunnel, his son, Brock, had been thrusting his out in a great hurry to join his father.

"Oh, father; you hurt me!" said his son.

"Well you hurt me!" said Blair Badger. "If you will race round like a mad March hare, you are obviously bound to hit somebody. Why can't you move round in a sensible fashion like everyone else? As it is I've been waiting here half the night for you to come out. When I say it's time to come out you should all come straight out, otherwise everything gets disorganised. What on earth are you all doing down there?"

His wife's voice came from deep in the burrow. "Now don't be silly, dear. We're trying to come out; but how *can* we with you standing right in the doorway?"

Blair Badger stood where he was quietly for a moment. As he stood he considered what to do and say. He could, for instance stay where he was and explain just why he was standing in the doorway. On the other hand the reason why he was standing in the doorway was to tell everyone to come out, which was what they all seemed determined to do in any case. Blair Badger could smell the sweet night air blowing into the tunnel entrance all round him from behind, and he thought of the stream at the bottom of the pasture tinkling and shining in the moonlit darkness.

He pulled his head out of his front door, turned round, and set off without more ado down the badger path that twisted across the heath.

He reached the stream, pushed through the nettles, and flopped down from the bank to the muddy edge to drink with the noise and sweet smell of the water in his ears and nose. It had been a hot stuffy day down in his home underground. Blair Badger sat for a time happily in the mud, listening to his beloved stream, and waiting also (since there was nothing else to do) for his family, who were, as usual, late. Blair Badger sighed.

"Yes," he said to the stream, "this is a wonderful place. I mustn't lose my temper over a little thing like the family being late. After all, life is easy here. Nothing ever really happens."

And the stream talked back to Blair Badger with its bubbling talk, agreeing with everything he said over and over again. That is the best thing about talking to a stream. It will never disagree with you.

But it happened that while Blair Badger was talking to the stream and wondering where his family had got to, and why they were always late and disorganised whereas he was cool, efficient and punctual, two other badgers were making their way towards him. They were making their way down the steep railway embankment that stood beyond the stream. They had travelled a long way and they were tired and rather fed up with each other, and so they were arguing—but in whispers in case anyone should hear them.

"Now look 'ere," one of them was whispering, "first you say you want a drink an' you must 'ave a drink, an' you can't go another step without a drink . . ."

"I do want a drink," whispered the other one, "but please be calm! I am tired; I am weary; yesterday I had no sleep . . ."

" 'Oo 'ad any sleep? I didn't 'ave no sleep yesterday, and I didn't 'ave none the day before neither. 'Oos talking about sleep? . . ."

By this time they were already right down by the stream, still arguing, when they heard another voice from the far side; a voice that spoke not in a whisper at all, and which sounded altogether rather cross;

"SO THERE YOU ARE," said the voice. "And what on earth are you whispering about? I've been waiting over here half the night for you."

The two strangers stopped whispering at

once, and fell silent for a moment with surprise. But the fact is that once you start arguing with someone you tend to go on arguing with everyone else, too.

" 'Ow do you mean you've been waiting for us 'alf the night? 'Oo told you we was coming anyway?" Now there was silence from the other bank. At last Blair Badger said:

"I beg your pardon, I'm sure. I thought you were my family, you see. My name is Blair Badger and I live here. May I ask who you are and where you come from?"

There was a snort from the other bank followed by a splashing sound as the two strangers waded across the stream.

"That's all right, mate. Let me introduce ourselves, and delighted to meet you, I'm sure," said the stranger as he plunged across the stream. "My name is Grimbart Dass, formerly of 'Ampstead 'Eath, London," he said, as he pulled himself out of the water, shook himself and soaked Blair Badger in the process. "And this 'ere," he added, as the second stranger pulled himself out of the water, "is Tasso, 'oo comes all the way from sunny Italy, and is, moreover, a well-known poet."

"*Molto piacere, signore,*" said Tasso politely, shaking the water from his fur, and soaking Blair Badger for the second time.

But Blair Badger was too interested to worry about being soaking wet.

"Good gracious," he said, "London! And Italy! But what on earth are you doing here?"

"Aha!" replied Grimbart Dass. "I'm very, very glad you asked that. In point of fact what we are doing here is to look for something to eat. In point of fact we are both very, very 'ungry. *Very* 'ungry," he added.

"Well," said Blair Badger. "Of course I don't know the sort of things you are used to in London; but here I'm afraid we just have simple food. For instance down here I quite often catch a vole or two. And then," he went on, warming to the subject of his home, "there are often rabbits about in the pasture up there, not to speak of mice, beetles and worms. There are plenty of herbs, too; dog's mercury, selfheal, tansy, wildmint. And then higher up you find moles, pheasant, and the odd pigeon's egg. And then, of course . . ."

But Tasso held up his paw.

"Enough!" he said. "Enough, *caro amico*

mio. Please I am hungry for food tonight, not for words. Your words speak of rabbit, of pigeon's egg, of, *dio mio*, of pheasant. Take us to them good friend; take us to them and speak not more, I beg you!"

And all Grimbert Dass said was: "Year!"

So the good Blair Badger, followed by his two new friends set off back up the hill without more ado, thinking of nothing but to find something really good to eat. He was, in fact, just turning round without stopping to mention to Tasso the path to take to get to a good blackberry thicket, when he bumped into his wife, who was coming with the children *downhill* to the stream and all but knocked Blair over in her haste. Blair Badger in his surprise forgot about his two friends for a moment, and was just pulling himself together either to tell his wife how long he had waited for her, or to ask her why she must rush about without looking where she was going, when his wife said:

"Blair; what have you been doing to get yourself soaking wet like that?"

And at that, of course, Blair remembered his two new friends and forgot about lateness and rushing about. He introduced everyone to everyone else, and Grimbart Dass and Tasso greeted Mrs. Blair Badger and the two children politely, if hungrily. After which they all set off for a night's rambling across the fir forest of Badger Hill. At the end of the night nobody was in the least bit hungry but simply, very, very tired. And as the first light of dawn grew in the summer sky, Blair Badger led Mrs. Blair Badger, the two children, Grimbart Dass and Tasso into the tunnel at the edge of the fir forest, and into the comfort of his underground home for a good long rest through the hot bright day.

NEWS OF MEN

WHEN Blair Badger woke the next evening it was with the feeling that things were not as they should be—or not as they usually were. He turned over in his fresh bracken bed and wondered why this should be.

Could it be something to do with his wife? He gave the heap of bracken beside him a little kick, and the heap of bracken grunted. No, it was nothing to do with her; she was asleep.

"The trouble is," he thought, "it's so warm down here. In fact, it's tremendously *hot*."

Blair Badger's sett was a small but pleasant place. It contained in the sandy depths of the hill two halls, a bedroom, a nursery for the children, and a number of passages that led between these and also led—rather vaguely since it was Blair Badger who had constructed them—to three different doorways to the outside world above. Usually it was cool in the summer and warm in winter; an ideal house.

But suddenly he felt so impossibly hot that he rolled right over again backwards towards the heap of bracken next to him, stretching out all four short legs as he did so. And the problem of why it was so hot was as suddenly solved for him; since the heap of bracken, speaking with a voice quite unlike his wife's but at the same time very irritably, said:

"For 'eaven's *sake*; sighing and rolling about and *kicking*; it's like trying to sleep on 'Ampstead 'Eath on the August Bank 'Oliday!"

And as Blair Badger saw the head of Grimbart Dass emerge from the pile of bracken he had thought to be his wife, he realised in less than a second the answer to his waking feeling of the unusualness of things, and why it was so hot in the bedroom of his home. Nor was he surprised when a second head appeared from among the bracken and said:

"*Buon giorno*" (which, as Blair correctly guessed, means 'good day' in Italian). And finally he wasn't in the least surprised when a moving about of bracken that all this involved disclosed his wife, Betsy—who said nothing because she was still fast asleep.

The three badgers who were all now quite awake, seeing Mrs. Blair so happily unaware of them, without any further words left the bedroom and made their way in single file down a sandy corridor until they came out at the doorway on the side of the hill.

"Well", said Grimbart Dass, "Tasso and me had better be on our way; very kind of you to put us up like that; very kind. I won't say we 'aven't enjoyed ourselves, because we 'ave. And," he added as he made to set off down the hill towards the stream, "please convey our thanks to your good lady, and say 'ow sorry we are that we didn't 'ave the opportunity to say goodbye to her."

"But, please," said Blair Badger, "Won't you stay to have some breakfast? There's surely no need to rush off! With another night of journeying ahead of you, you should at least start with something in your stomachs."

The two travelling badgers looked at each other for a long moment.

"Our host is most kind," murmured Tasso at last.

"Of course," said Grimbart, "it's true that we would make better time if we had a snack before we started. . . ."

"Perhaps, as you say, just a small snack . . ." agreed Tasso.

"Well, as you insist . . ." said Grimbart weakly.

"I do," said Blair firmly.

The three of them set off into the forest, nosing hungrily at the ground. Blue night deepened above them, and the forest was very dark indeed as they made their way in single file at first up and down the hilly ground along the badger path. They came out of the fir plantation at a place where the old wire-netting fence had been pushed over, and passed into thickets of young chestnut trees with clearings where brambles, nettles, dock and dog's mercury had grown and twined and stood higher than they did. Beyond lay a small road that they crossed with great caution; and up a bank they came into an orchard running down into the valley. They passed among the neat ranks of trees, making a feast of half-ripe windfall apples, maggots and all. Beyond the orchard lay a rough pasture where they startled the sheep as they grazed or slept with snorts and badger-shouts. So they came down a sudden steep bank where the roots of trees twisted among moss; and at the bottom of the bank they flopped down at the very edge of a river that flowed slowly in deep pools, immensely black in the darkness. Here they lay on their backs among nettles and gazed into the night above them quietly for a time. Then Blair Badger said:

"You were going to tell me why you are travelling."

"Yes," said Grimbart Dass. He rolled over on to his feet, and pushing into the rushes at the muddy edge of the river, he took a long drink. He came out again backwards, and, turning round, said impressively:

"I'll tell you in one word why Tasso and me are travelling: *Men. Men* is why we are travelling."

He made his way to a comfortable clump of nettles and sat down to gaze at the moving black river. "For years and years," he continued, "generation after generation, in fact, my family has had to put up with men. And put up with them we have. Men with sticks, men with spades, men with guns, men with traps, men with railway trains, and men with

motor cars—But you know what men are!"
As it happened, all Blair Badger knew about
men was that the farmer who lived in the next
valley occasionally stopped up some of his
doorways, which was irritating and pointlessly
rude so far as Blair Badger was concerned—but no more than that. However he
replied: "Oh, yes!" because it seemed to be
expected of him.

"Well, then," continued Grimbart Dass.
"That's it, you see! Tasso and I decided that
we must get right away from it; start again;
take to the road; find a new place; make a
clean break with the past, and . . . and . . . well,
start travelling!" he ended rather lamely.

"I see," said Blair Badger. There was a
short silence after this as Blair thought it all
over. "But," he said at last, "what about the
winter?"

"'Ow d'you mean, what about winter?"
said Grimbart. "What *about* winter? I never
mentioned winter. We weren't discussing
winter. We were discussing why it was that
Tasso and I . . ."

"Yes, yes, yes," said Tasso. "Our kind host
is right, you know. We must find somewhere

to stay before winter comes. Somewhere . . . somewhere something like this," he added quietly.

There was a silence.

Grimbart Dass looked at Tasso.

Tasso looked at Grimbart Dass.

"Look 'ere," said Grimbart finally. "My mate 'ere and I was just wondering if we might spend the winter somewhere round about 'ere. What do you think?"

"Why," replied Blair, "so far as I am concerned it is an excellent plan. I thought you were keen to get on your way. But there is one thing. You see all the land round here belongs to Lady Grey. You will have to ask her permission, and, well, we won't see her before Lammas-tide; and she's well, I mean, it's rather difficult . . ."

But we must now leave Blair, Grimbart and Tasso talking unhungrily among the nettles in the dawn, and get quietly back to Blair's house. Dawn found Mrs. Blair Badger tidying up there and changing the beds. Her two

children were out, as they were, it seemed
these nights, more often than not. As the lark
rose whistling into the lightening sky above
the pasture and the cock crowed in the valley,
Betsy Blair dragged out the bracken from the
bed-chamber and pulled it out of the house
altogether. Then she tore off fresh green
fronds from the thicket nearby, gathered
them under her chin, and made her way slowly backwards into the house and down the
tunnel to the bedchamber.

Making your way in and out of places
backwards with bracken tucked under your
chin as badgers often do requires thought and
concentration, so Betsy got rather a shock
when a voice said very loudly:

"View Halloo! Lovely mornin'!"

Betsy got such a shock, in fact she dropped
the bedding she had carefully carried to her
front door all over the path. And she turned to
find herself face to face with a magnificently
large and somewhat formidable-looking
chestnut brown badger.

"Just tidyin' up, are you?" said this newcomer, looking absently at the pile of bracken
at Betsy's feet, which had now got into a mud-

dle with some old bedding she had previously thrown out.

"Oh, good morning, Lady Grey," said Mrs. Blair. "You gave me a surprise."

"Mornin' Betsy," said Lady Grey. "Often seem to do that—give people surprises, I mean; don't know why it should be. Blair about?" she added, walking confidently down onto the mixed up pile of old and new bedding, and gazing and sniffing enquiringly into the doorway. Mrs Blair explained to Lady Grey that her husband was still out.

"No matter," said the other. "No matter at all. Just wanted to remind you both that it's Lammas-tide, and invite you to the party at my place as usual. I expect Blair has forgotten all about it."

Mrs. Blair agreed that he almost certainly had, and thanked Lady Grey for the invitation and for reminding them.

"You see," she said, "We had visitors." And she explained about the two travelling badgers. "Of course," she said, "I'm sure they won't be staying long; I should think they have probably gone off by now. But it was rather interesting having them about, and hearing a little of the world," she added wistfully.

"Good!" said Lady Grey, sternly. "Sooner they're off the better; don't want a lot of strangers messing about on the property. Blair's a good fellow; but innocent, if I may say so; doesn't know a thing about the world, that's his trouble. But let me warn you, Betsy Blair, you'ld best be rid of them. You can't trust Italians further than you can throw 'em," she said, moving her impressive looking shoulders as though she were enjoying the idea. "And Blair ought to know that Londoners are the worst of the lot; shockin' creatures, the whole lot of 'em."

"I'm sure you're right, of course," said Mrs. Blair. "All the same," she added, "it was fun to meet them." Lady Grey relented a little.

"Tell you what," she said. "If they're still around—which I hope they're not, of course—you can invite 'em to the Lammas-tide party. But after that—off they go. Is that all clear?"

"Oh, thank you!" said Mrs. Blair, obviously very pleased with this.

"Don't mention it, Betsy," said Lady Grey

kindly; "don't mention it. Anyway, must be off now. See you this evening."

And only when she was already half way back into the forest she turned and said, "By the way; heard the news?"

"What news?" asked Mrs. Blair, interestedly.

"Shockin' thing, really," said Lady Grey.

"What is?" said Betsy Blair.

"It's the *Men*," replied Lady Grey over her shoulder; "building again; dashed scandal, the way they do it without so much as a 'by your leave'!"

"But what are they building?" shouted Betsy Blair.

"Houses," shouted back her ladyship, "Hundreds of 'em. Anyway, can't stop now," she added as she disappeared among the trees. "I'll tell you this evening at the party."

Betsy Blair thus went back to her tidying up, feeling worried at the thought of Lady Grey's strange news; and at the same time cheerful at the thought of the coming party. As it happened she was thinking about doing a spot of building herself. She finished with the beds and went down into the house, which she had decided to enlarge in view of the fact that there were guests about.

It took her some time to decide where she would dig out a new guest-room and how it should be arranged, and she thought a little enviously of Lady Eleanor Grey's fine house, Grey Hatch, where the Lammas-tide party was to be held that night as it was every year. By the time she was out of the sett again with her building completed it was already early morning, and the sun was shining on the feathery crowns of the fir trees. She sat down for some time shaking her long head as she considered how visitors, men's buildings and the Lammas-tide party all seemed suddenly to be happening all at once.

3

LAMMAS-TIDE

TASSO and Grimbart Dass awoke that evening feeling much refreshed and in much better spirits altogether. Grimbart Dass lay on his back in the new guest room, and twiddled his toes cheerfully, while Tasso combed with his claws and licked at his sleek coat. Tasso was a small but handsome badger, and was always most careful about his appearance. On the other hand none of these things could be said about Grimbart Dass.

"'Ow kind," said Grimbart Dass as he leant forward to scratch his stomach, "'Ow very kind of Lady Grey to invite us to 'er party. She sounds a most pleasant lady it seems to me."

"I was thinking just the same myself," agreed Tasso as he worked with his claws at a very small tangle of shining black hair where a bramble had made a knot on the previous night.

"It seems to me," went on Grimbart, "that if we can make a good impression on 'er ladyship this evening, we might persuade her to let us stay after all."

"Exactly," replied Tasso. "That's why I am tidying myself up," he added, looking pointedly at his friend.

Grimbart turned over on to his stomach.

"In all probability she is a charming gentle creature," he went on, "and obviously very 'ospitable. At least that is 'ow I imagine 'er. She might well be glad to have a couple of badgers-of-the-world around like ourselves, with brain and initiative."

"I think you may well be right," said Tasso. If one shows oneself to be charming and cultured," he continued, "and to possess a certain elegance, one may melt her heart. I shall read her a few of my poems," he added.

Grimbart Dass sat up suddenly as though he had been stung.

"Look 'ere," he said, "I think it might be just as well if you let me 'andle this. They can be funny people, the English aristocracy, you know. Of course I'm not saying anything against your poems. . . ." This might have developed into an argument, but luckily Blair Badger's head appeared in the doorway of the guest room.

"Good evening," he said, "all ready?" Grimbart Dass jumped to his feet and pulled a bracken frond from his head. "Good evening, Blair," he said. "Of course we're ready."

The four badgers set off in single file through the fir forest. Grey Hatch was at a far side of the forest, and a good mile away. But they were all anxious to arrive and went at a good pace. As they went Grimbart caught up with Blair, and nudged him.

"Very nice to be going to the Lammas-tide party," he said.

"I think you'll enjoy it," said Blair. "We do it well here."

"Year" said Grimbart. Do you have it often?" Blair looked at him surprised.

"Once a year," he said, "at Lammas-tide."

"Oh, year, naturally," said Grimbart.

They walked on a little way, until at last Grimbart said suddenly:

"Look 'ere, mate; would you be good enough to tell me one thing: What *is* Lammas-tide?"

"Lammas-tide?" replied Blair in surprise. "Why, my dear fellow, Lammas-tide is the best remembered of our old country festivals. It is the festival of first-fruits, when the blackberries are beginning to ripen and the spiders are spinning their webs among the brambles in the mornings, and the apples are turning red upon the trees, and the night-jars whirr in the woods, and . . . Ah, here we are: Grey Hatch!"

They had arrived at the great plantation of ancient oaks and beeches where Grey Hatch lay. Under those great quiet trees the four visitors became silent, and with a certain apprehensiveness they stopped before the massive sandy doorway that opened under a hollybush—the main gateway into Grey Hatch. They paused in front of the door.

"This it?" said Grimbart Dass. Blair Badger nodded.

"Shall we go in, then?" said Grimbart Dass.

"Oh, do go on Blair," said Betsy Blair.

"I'm *going* on," he replied. He put his head into the doorway enquiringly, coughed, and said:

all we go in, then?" said Grimbart Dass.

"Anyone at home?"

All four of them put their noses in at the doorway, and there was a loud snort from behind them.

"What the dickens is goin' on?" said a loud voice, and the four of them withdrew their noses from the doorway and turned almost like one badger to face the handsome and chestnut-brown Lady Grey.

"Oh, it's you Blair," said Lady Grey. "Well, of course I'm at home. Why on earth should I invite you to a party and then go out? Evenin' Betsy. Nice to see you."

"Good evening, Eleanor," said Mrs. Blair.

Introductions were made and the party set out for the Lammas-tide feast without more ado. As they moved through the country together the spirit of the festival gripped them and they made their way among the dark woods with increasing noise and gaiety. For so it has been for years beyond all counting that the badgers have felt this same spirit creep upon them that makes them gather together to celebrate the season of ripeness at the end of the year, when their homelands will be full of the harvest that has been all summer growing, and will be ready to eat and eat against the thin months of winter ahead. Then, more than at any other time, the badgers know that their homelands are theirs by rights more ancient than any that men know. For badgers were celebrating Lammas-tide with screams and boisterous games before there were ever men in these lands, and in the far-off times when the wolf-packs ran silently among the trees. And now, although men have come and made farms, and farms have become villages, and villages cities; and although the men killed the last wolf more than four hundred years ago, the badgers are still masters of their ancient homes. So they celebrate the end of summer in the night-woods that are full of moths and mice and sleeping birds.

That night, too, the five badgers celebrated as all festivals should be celebrated; as though, in fact, it was the first, last and best Lammas-tide ever known. They feasted. Beetles and worms, grubs and grass seeds were consumed. Fallen pigeons' eggs were licked up and bluebell bulbs were dug up. A hedgehog was discovered, pulled open and devoured, leaving the prickle case neatly on the ground. Blackberries were pulled from the bramble, noses lifted delicately to avoid being pricked. They danced. They clambered and galloped round a fallen tree where a thick bramble grew, pushing each other from the tree or diving suddenly through the bramble with shouts and songs, until at last exhausted, they all lay about helpless with badger laughter; and until they became too tired to laugh even, and simply lay while bats circled and dipped above them and spiders spun great cart-wheel webs among the bramble.

Grimbart Dass sat up suddenly and addressed his hostess:

"Your ladyship," he began, "on behalf of my friend and myself I should like to thank you for a most enjoyable evening; and I should also like to ask you if . . ."

"Not at all, not at all," said Lady Grey, also sitting up. "I expect you will both be on your way soon, hey?"

Now Tasso sat up.

"Madam," he said, "You are kindness itself. And it is for that reason among others that I have the courage to ask of you a great favour—a favour that, should you grant it, would show two simple creatures that hospitality far from being dead, is even more . . ."

"That's all right," said Lady Grey, "no need to make a long speech out of it. I can see that you're gentlemen and decent fellows and so on. I know what you want. You'd like to see over Grey Hatch before you go." Now Blair Badger sat up.

"Oh, yes," he said to his friends. You must see Grey Hatch you know!"

And then Betsy Blair sat up.

"And also, Eleanor," she said, "you were going to tell me your news this morning about the men's buildings." Grimbart Dass tried again.

"You see, your ladyship, we would like to make so bold as to ask you . . ."

"Good grief," said Lady Grey; "Nearly forgot; shockin' thing; makes my hair stand on end when I think about it. Come with me everyone; I'll *show* you the news!" And she set off through the wood without further ado. Blair and Betsy scrambled up and followed her at once, and there seemed to be nothing that the two travelling badgers could do except follow as well.

"You must ask her!" whispered Tasso. "You are not asking her!"

"I am asking her," whispered back Grimbart. "I keep trying to ask her. And anyway, what's wrong with you asking her?"

So they followed the others through the woods getting deeper and deeper into their argument, and when Lady Grey, Blair and Betsy stopped at the edge of the forest Grimbart and Tasso were so involved that they went on right past the others, still arguing.

"I know I said I wanted to 'andle this," Grimbart was saying, "but I didn't mean that I was going to do everything; and anyway she makes me feel shy too, as it 'appens."

"Halt!" said Lady Grey sternly. And Grimbart and Tasso halted.

"Look!" said Lady Grey. And they looked. They looked down and out into the valley and across to the great man's City of Canterbury, which lay at some distance. Or it had lain at some distance. But now, as the five badgers gazed short-sightedly into the night, a dog began to bark in the valley just below them and strange smells floated into their noses—the smells of smoke and of petrol, of cooking and of dust: the smells of man.

"Good gracious to me!" said Blair Badger, "They've moved the city nearer!"

"Don't be a fool, Blair," said Lady Grey. " 'Course they haven't moved it nearer. They've made it bigger. The valley's full of houses and roads right up to the hill here now. I know, because I've been down there."

"What a peculiar smell," said Betsy Blair.

"Foul, isn't it?" agreed Lady Grey. "Completely ruins the place. And only a short walk from Grey Hatch, too."

"What a terrible thing; don't you think so?" said Blair turning to the two travellers.

These two looked at one another slowly. Tasso gave a long sigh.

"Of course," said Grimbart slowly, "you know what this means?"

"Yes," said Lady Grey. "I know what it means. It means that this part of the property is completely ruined and spoiled as far as I'm concerned. Its disgustin'."

"No, no, your ladyship," replied Grimbart quietly. "It means much more than that I can tell you, and so can Tasso 'ere. It means that you may 'ave to leave 'ere. It means that you may 'ave to take to the road, like Tasso and me. It means that if you stay 'ere too long there'll be nothing left of you but shiving brushes!"

"Shaving brushes?" repeated Blair in a shocked voice.

"Year," said Grimbart; "shiving brushes! You don't think they'll stop down there do you? Because I can tell you they won't. They'll be up 'ere scaring the mice and pulling up the bluebells, and setting traps, and digging out holes, and on and on and on . . . Oh, well! I suppose Tasso and me had better be on our way. Goodbye to you all, thanks for having us and good luck!"

As the two travelling badgers set off back into the forest the sky began to lighten with dawn. The others watched them, and as they watched the noise of the first motor car of the day started up in the valley, and in the quietness the motor seemed amazingly loud, like the roars of some heartless, thoughtless animal. By the time the noise had died away Tasso and Grimbart Dass had almost disappeared into the shadows of the still dark forest. Then the powerful voice of Lady Grey suddenly was heard.

"Just a minute, you two," she shouted; "want to talk to you!"

4

GREY HATCH

GREY Hatch was large and rambling due to the various additions that had been made to it by different members of the Grey family in different directions as the fancy had taken them. And since it lay under a grove of oak trees of even greater age than the house itself, the noble and massive roots of these trees ran across ceilings and down walls, or occasionally occurred as pillars in the middle of rooms, lending tremendous strength and dignity to the whole structure. It was, in fact, as Lady Grey explained to Grimbart and Tasso, when she led them into the main hall from which tunnels branched to left and right above and below leading to different galleries and chambers, a traditional half-timbered wealden house, comfortable and spacious.

Blair and Mrs. Blair had set off already for home as the day was already beginning. Although their two children of the year were really scarcely children any longer and spent a lot of the time by themselves, Blair and Mrs. Blair felt rather more anxious about them than usual in view of the news of the arrival of men so close to Badger Hill, and hoped to find them back at their home.

"Now then," said Lady Grey to Grimbart and Tasso, "How about it?"

" 'Ow about what?" said Grimbart.

"Givin' up all this nonsense," said Lady Grey.

"All what nonsense?" said Grimbart.

"Why all this travellin' nonsense," said Lady Grey. I'll tell you how it is," she went on, warming to her subject. "The thing is this; we need creatures like you; badgers of the world; creatures of brain and initiative. There aren't many of us here, as you know. Blair and Betsy are a nice couple, of course; but—well, their children don't know much about the world either. What I'm trying to say, is, there's an old badger sett right on the far side of the hill here; winter's comin' on and so on. Well, why don't you? Glad to have you around, especially if things turn out to be anything like as serious as you say they are."

Grimbart Dass looked unhappy. He looked down at his stomach, and scratched it with a paw.

"We'ld like to stay, of course," he said, "but . . . but . . ." Tasso held up his paw.

"Madam," he said, "allow me to tell you the story of my life."

Tasso began, in his soft Italian voice, to tell of his birth on an Italian hillside in the mountains. He told of his life with his parents, of the bright blue skies of his home, and of the hot days, and warm nights.

Then he told how he had been captured while still quite young by some hunters who had taken him alive back to their village in a sack. They had decided to shoot him at first, but it happened that a circus was travelling through the village. Since Tasso had always been small the circus people thought that he was younger than he really was, and so one of them bought him to try to train him, and took Tasso with him across the Alps and through France. Tasso described his journeys with the circus—the nightly roars of the crowds of people at the show, the grinding and banging of the great circus lorries along the roads of

Europe—and his listeners shivered. He described his life as a circus animal. His owner had not been unkind by the standards of men, but the food was dull, poor stuff to a badger, and much of Tasso's time was spent locked in a small box. It was there that he had first occupied himself with composing poetry, during the long, dark hours as his owner moved across the continent. His poetry told, he said, of the open air of his Italian homeland and of the pleasures of wandering among the parched herbs of the hot Tuscan hills in summer. Finally, Tasso told how his owner had come to England, had taken a job with a fair, and how the fair had come to Hampstead Heath near London for August Bank Holiday.

By then Tasso was a misery to himself and a nuisance to his owner, who, on the day of the fair when he was especially busy, left the padlock unlocked on Tasso's box. Tasso had grown so used to his life there in a miserable fashion that he might have stayed there in its comforting darkness, ready to defend himself against any prying and foolish dogs or men who might have tried to torment him. But it was a particularly hot day, and the smells from the warm plants and trees of the heath reminded him so strongly of his home, that he all at once decided to make a dash for them. He ran desperately among men's legs and under the hot wheels of caravans and lorries, with shouts and barks in his ears. After a time he realised that he was on his own, but he didn't stop running until he came to a badger sett, and he bolted straight down this like a frightened rabbit.

"It happened," ended Tasso, "that this was the home of one who was to become my good friend, Grimbart—but please!" he added, "there is no need for tears!"

For Eleanor Grey was weeping quietly, her fine chestnut-brown shoulders moving up and down as she sobbed. Tasso moved over and put his arm round her.

"Come!" he said. "The story has a happy ending. Grimbart and I became friends, talked things over, and decided to travel as far as we need to get away from men. Now, madam, you will understand why we will not stay here."

"But what am I to do," said Lady Grey.

Grimbart Dass himself was looking gloomy.

"What are any of us to do?" he said. "It may not be too bad 'ere for you. Mabye they won't come up 'ere too much. Listen," he added, "why don't you come along with Tasso and me this evening as far as Blair's house? You'll feel better with friends." So it was agreed and the three of them set out over Badger Hill even before sunset. Lady Grey had recovered herself by then.

"Sorry about all that snivellin'," she said as they made their way through the forest where the last sunlight turned the fir trees to blue and gold.

"Please," said Tasso, putting his arm about her shoulders again, "there is no need for an apology."

"In any case, as I say," said Grimbart, "they may not come up here too much."

"One must not lose heart," said Tasso.

"And besides," said Grimbart, "you may well be safer off than what we are."

"Indeed," said Tasso, "travelling is a dangerous business at the best of times."

So they made their way to Blair Badger's little house with words of comfort that cheered them all up, the comforters as well as the comforted, for it usually happens that cheering someone else up is a most effective way of cheering up yourself.

"Now," said Grimbart as they approached Blair's sett, "Tasso and me will just say good-bye to Blair and 'is missus, and then we'll . . ." Then he stopped. They all stopped and smelled. Then they looked. As they gazed with short-sighted badger eyes, they could scarcely believe what they saw, and they moved nearer, sniffing with clever noses to make sure of it.

There were many smells in the air—smells that would have told them much even if they had not seen anything at all. There was the smell of freshly dug sandy earth; the smell of wet concrete and of iron; the smell of frightened badgers; and above all everywhere the smell of man himself. But more they could see with their eyes. A new fence had been put round the edge of the woods that day, and posts for the fence had been placed and concreted into place right through the roof of Blair's house. The entrance had fallen in, and the roof of the new guest room had also collapsed with the digging and stamping of men and their machines; while the post itself had been concreted into place almost exactly where the hall had lain underground.

There was, in fact, no house left worth talking about, and certainly no house left worth living in. Grimbart pulled himself together with a shrug and a snort.

"Come on," he said to Tasso, "let's see what we can find."

The two friends began to move round the ground near the house with the greatest care, heads moving left and right as they sniffed; but they could neither see, smell, nor hear any sign of the Blairs other than the frightened smell, that made them uneasy themselves.

"Anyway," said Grimbart, "there's no smell of dogs either."

They decided to try further back into the wood. After they had nosed there for a while, Tasso gave a sudden grunt and Grimbart quickly joined him.

"See," said Tasso, "they went away— here." And sure enough the smell and scattered leaves and paw marks of badgers in a hurry led away into the woods, and started from a small and disused back entrance to what had been Blair's house. When Grimbart and Tasso got back to Lady Grey, they found her still standing exactly where they had left her, and still staring at the ruins of Blair's house.

"Gone," she said, when they told her what they had found, "Who's gone?"

"Blair and Betsy," said Grimbart. "They got away; cleared off; done a flit; vamoosed; 'opped it." Lady Grey recovered herself.

"Gone where?" she said.

"We don't exactly know yet," said Grimbart, "but there's signs into the forest."

"Don't know? Well, good heavens man, we must find out! This is no time to stand chattering! Show me the scent!"

And they were off into the forest again, moving quickly as their clever noses followed the trail of the Blairs. At first it moved this way and that, as if in a panic, although always deeper into the forest. But after a time the trail became more settled and less frightened, and led after a sudden turn almost straight, through undergrowth, over hill and hollow, up towards the heights of the Badger Hill forest, where the woods grew deeper and darker and the undergrowth grew thicker and thornier. The trail was especially easy for the badgers to follow now, for Blair had had to force his way through dense undergrowth, over or under fallen and rotting trees, and had left a kind of tunnel behind him as he went. At one point the trail crossed a small stream—which they almost fell into so hidden was it by thick grasses—and soon it looped about the very summit of Badger Hill, and then plunged into fern that quite hid the opening of an underground passage.

And here at last Lady Grey stopped and turned to wait for her two companions who were a little way behind her. As they came up, rather puffing and panting after this long hard chase, she said:

"For once in his life Blair seems to have shown some sense. This is the old sett I mentioned to you yesterday at Grey Hatch. They must be here."

Grimbart Dass looked about him, still panting a little, at the fronds of fern and long grass that sprang round the twisted roots of old trees.

"Quite a place," he said at last.

Tasso nodded: "An ancient place," he said, "and a wild one."

"Hush!" said Lady Grey, and she put her nose into the chalky entrance to the tunnel among the ferns, and called:

"Good brother Blair! Come forth I say! It is your dear comrades who call you!"

THERE was no reply to Lady Grey's call. She turned, and with a curt: "Follow me!" to the others, she pushed into the tunnel in the chalk. Tasso and Grimbart followed as they had been told to do, and almost at once the tunnel opened out into a great chamber built of slabs of stone—an immense place to the badgers. Lady Grey called again:

"Blair, are you there?"

And from the blackness of the chamber the strange voice of echo answered them: "Blair . . . there . . . Blair . . . there . . ."

This was enough for Grimbart and Tasso, who turned about like a single badger, and collided at the entrance to the tunnel they had entered by.

"Oof," said Grimbart.

"Woof," said Tasso. And the voice of echo repeated 'oof . . . woof' several times, just as if it had been trying to get out itself.

"What the dickens is goin' on?" said Lady Grey sternly. "Come back here both of you!"

Sheepishly Grimbart and Tasso came back. She now made her way across the stone chamber and down into the tunnel at the far side that made its way down into the chalk. They followed her in single file, as they went down into a maze of tunnels that ran this way and that like a puzzle.

But the scent trail was strong again, nor was it long before their shouts for Blair were answered by Blair himself. Soon they were together again: Blair, Betsy, Grimbart, Tasso and Lady Grey. Indeed they were very much together again, for they met in a widened part of the tunnel that was only just large enough for them all to stand. There was no complaint about the crowding, however, for they were all delighted to have found one another again safe and sound. All five of them made their way now, led by Blair himself, along a further tunnel that followed an underground stream tinkling through the chalk hill in the darkness until it came out on the hillside. And there they stopped to drink and eat a little grass in the cool night, while Blair explained to the others what a terrible fright he had had when his home had been destroyed. The two children had been out—but that had been just as well, on the whole. Blair and Betsy had waited at first quietly when they heard the noise and tread of the men above them. They had waited until the spades had begun to thump into the earth over their heads, and the sandy ceiling of the hall had begun to rain upon their heads—because they had had no way of knowing what the men were doing, and had hoped they would simply go away again. So at the last moment they galloped along the crumbling passage, and up out into the wood.

"The rest of our journey you know," ended Blair simply. And the others nodded and snuffled, as they each thought over all that had happened to them since the carefree Lammas-tide feast they had celebrated together only the night before.

"You were right to warn us, Grimbart," said Blair at last. "I shall never go back to that old place now. Betsy and I will stay here for the winter anyway."

"And I will stay here with you," said Lady

Grey. "For the time bein' anyhow it may be safer for the three of us to stick together. Well," she said, turning to Grimbart and Tasso, "I suppose you two will be on your way, what? Almost wish I was comin' with you; but I can't leave Badger Hill. There've been Greys here since well before the Conquest, and well before the conquest before that, and before the one before that, too; and I'm not goin' to be the one that leaves."

Then the little Italian badger spoke:

"Madam," he said, "or may I call you Eleanor? You know my story, and how it was that Grimbart and myself were travellers. Most of my life has been spent in travelling; but now I have had enough of it. I am ready to stay with you, Eleanor, whatever the future holds—if you will have me!" And the redoubtable Lady Eleanor Grey squirmed the fine muscles of her brown shoulders in a manner that was almost girlish.

"Oh, Tasso," she replied, "you know that I'm yours!" And they kissed.

"Well I'm blowed!" said Grimbart Dass.

"My friend," said Tasso, "you see that I

cannot come with you. But I wish you all luck as you go."

"Go?" said Grimbart, "Go? 'Oose talking about going? I'm not going. I'm staying. When I think of Blair's 'ouse and all of you stuck 'ere with that mob," he said, nodding violently in the direction of the city. "I could no more go than fly. I don't feel like travellin' any more. I feel like stayin'. And if stayin' means fightin' " he added savagely, "I feel like fightin' an' all!" They were all silent for a time after that, as they each thought their own thoughts.

"Come on," said Blair suddenly. "We must celebrate." So they chased off together through the dense heights of Badger Wood, and ate and sang more wholeheartedly even than they had done on the previous night. They raced to the very summit of the hill, where among alder and chestnut trees they could see right out over Canterbury as the lights of the City reflected in the cloudy night sky. They looked at it from the top of their silent fortress until suddenly, drop by drop, it began to rain—and then to pour.

They galloped down into the forest,

h, Tasso," she replied, "you know that I'm yours!

scattering in all directions, shouting silly remarks to one another that were only half heard as the rain smacked and drummed on the leaves and dry ground. When at last the rain stopped, the five badgers, now weary, crawled or shambled into any dry place they could find in thickets or in holes, and fell asleep as the grey dawn of a cloudy day rose over Badger Hill and over the sleeping City of Canterbury beyond it.

AUTUMN had come. Across the countryside of the Kentish Downs the farmers dipped their sheep for the winter, and from their orchards picked the beautiful red and golden apples and cherries, which they sold at high prices to the men from the cities. Down in the valley at the foot of Badger Hill the men in the new houses lifted the first of their first crop of potatoes from their new gardens, and lit bonfires to burn up the rubbish of summer; bonfires that smouldered and glowed sometimes all through the night, and sent thin smoke up the hill where its strange sweet and bitter smells sometimes entered the noses of badgers and made them uneasy.

But the badgers, too, were busy with autumn that filled the night woods with new wonders. The tawny owl hooted as he searched the clearings, and the moths of the season had appeared—the Brindled Green, the Beaded Chestnut, the Yellowline Quaker, the Mallow and the Streak—and sucked through the nights at the sweetness of the ivy flowers that had begun to show.

The woods were full of the harvest of the year—elderberries, mushrooms, hips, haws, blackberries, hazelnuts. As the season advanced conkers and acorns began to thump on the floor of the woods, and later still beechmast and sweet chestnuts fell beside them. The badgers ate and ate. They ate all night and quite often came out during the day to eat more. Their stomachs grew tight with food and still they were hungry. Their coats grew thicker and glossier, and their shoulders became rounder and heavier, and still they were hungry.

And they were busy with other things too. As men and dogs slept through the lengthening nights down in the valley, the badgers on the hill above men's houses worked secretly. Their plans were made, as all plans must be made, before winter comes. Blair's and Betsy's two children of the year had decided to spend winter across the hill in a small sett they had made there. They were almost adult now; at least they were old enough to be scornful of the fears of their parents and their parents' friends. And in any case they wanted to be away and on their own. They came back occasionally to find out how things were going with these others, and sometimes they were visited by these others to find out how things were going with them.

Meanwhile the five badgers worked at their new winter quarters in the old sett on the heights of the hill, which they had begun to call 'First and Last Earth'. It was, as Grimbart Dass had remarked, quite a place. And it was, as Tasso had remarked, an ancient place. This very top of the hill had been used by both men and badgers in times gone by. On it men had made in ancient times a tomb for some warrior of old, and under it badgers long since dead had constructed a place to live. Whether man or badger had been the first there was beyond Blair or Lady Grey or anyone else to decide. But it was clear that both men and badgers had left it unvisited for many, many years.

The hill there was of chalk and hard to dig even for a badger's claws. On the other hand, once dug, the halls and passages were as strong as a castle. It was an eerie place, too. Once, in the course of digging and clearing the old setts, Tasso came upon an old badger burial place and pulled out of it the skull of a badger. At another time Blair came upon the skull of a man. And Grimbart Dass, while digging about, found an ancient dagger, green with age. He examined it curiously, and then threw it out with the other rubbish at his new front door.

But the badgers became used to the place, and its very wildness and deserted air gave them the feeling of being safe. When all was finished it was a different place to the one they had come to. Outside, round the hill, were the piles of earth and chalk which they had dug and cleared. Inside, all was clean, tidy and pleasant. Doorways connected with halls, halls with tunnels, and tunnels with bedchambers. All in all the place was as fine a fortress as a creature could wish for.

Life was pleasant. As the badgers grew fat with the autumn food they spent their leisure time in visits to one another and in romps through the woods. There were times, indeed, when life seemed almost too pleasant. It was on just such an evening that Grimbart Dass was the first to come out. Blue and warm, it was like an evening that had been missed out from summer somehow, and had become fitted into the later part of the year to avoid losing it altogether—an evening, in fact, of what is called Saint Martin's Summer. Grimbart sniffed the air as he came out, but he didn't take much notice of it. He felt safe. Perhaps a bit too safe. He came out and sat for a moment at his doorway, scratched himself and snufflled. He looked around him as the forest darkened in twilight, and wondered what to do. He sighed.

"Oh, dearie me," he said.

He gazed round at the lovely woods, sniffling in the warm, bitter smells which they sent into his nose.

"Dearie, dearie, me," he said.

Presently, Tasso and Blair came by, and hailed him as they came:

"Hullo there, Grimbart!"

"Evening, Grimbart!"

"Lovely evening, hey?"

"Been warm in our place today."

"Was in ours, too."

"Really?"

"Still, best time of the year, I must say."

"Oh, absolutely!"

They paused and looked at Grimbart.

"Hullo," he said at last.

The two others looked surprised.

"Something wrong, old chap?" asked Blair.

"No, no; everything's just fine," said Grimbart gloomily.

"You are feeling well, I hope?" said Tasso.

"Yes, oh, yes," said Grimbart. "I'm feeling just fine."

"Well, then," said Tasso, "how about coming for a bit of a stroll?"

"Thanks all the same," said Grimbart. "I think I'll just stay here and do a bit of cleaning or something." His two friends were not sure what to do with him in this mood, and at last they went off, assuring him he should catch them up if he felt like it later.

After they had gone, Grimbart sat for a bit longer.

"Dearie me," he said. "Oh dear, oh dear, oh dearie me!"

After he had said 'oh dear' and 'dearie me' a few more times, Lady Grey appeared.

"Evenin' Grimbart," she said. "Well, how about it?"

" 'Ow about *what?*"

"Catchin' up the others," said Lady Grey; "Havin' a bit of a ramble; eatin'!" she added enthusiastically. Grimbart turned a mournful face upon her.

"No thanks," he said, "if it's all the same to you, I think I'll just do a few jobs here, or something." He looked round him vaguely. "If it's all the same to you," he added gloomily.

Lady Grey looked surprised. "What sort of jobs?" she asked with her usual directness.

"Oh . . . cleaning up and that," replied the other vaguely. At last Lady Grey, too, left; and when he heard the padding footsteps of Betsy Blair approaching, he felt he could not stand up to another conversation like that at all. So he hurriedly made his way back into his sett before she came into view. It wasn't long before she went away again, and he felt able to say a few more 'oh dears' to himself without being overheard. The trouble was, he told himself, that he was bored. He gazed round his rather untidy hall and sighed.

"What's the point, anyway?" he said. "That's what I want to know." He ambled outside again, sat down, scratched, and looked about him. "The country!" he said bitterly; "Very pretty, of course; no-one's denying that; but dull; dull as ditchwater!"

He wandered up the steep slope of the summit of the hill and sat down at the top, where he could see out over the city to the lights that showed orange in the sky. Presently he heard the quiet bark of a badger calling to him through the woods. He didn't reply at first, because he didn't feel much like talking to anyone. But the barks were repeated and at last Grimbart replied. In a short time he was joined on the hilltop by one of Blair's two children, Brock, who greeted him with enthusiasm:

"Evening, Mr. Dass."

"Evening, son."

"All alone, Mr. Dass?"

"I was," replied Grimbart.

"What are you doing?"

"I was just thinking," said Grimbart,

"about the times I spent in the wide world."

"Were you really?" said Brock respectfully.

"Yes," replied Grimbart, "I was."

"Gosh!" said Blair's son.

"Yes," said Grimbart, feeling a little better. "I was thinking what a good thing it is to 'ave a bit of experience of the world; see a bit of life; travel; adventure; excitement!"

"Gosh" said Blair's son again. By now Grimbart Dass was feeling much better.

"Oh, yes," he went on, "I could tell you a story or two!"

He laughed, a short, bitter laugh. He waited for a moment in order to give Blair's son a chance to say 'Gosh', or 'Good heavens, Mr. Dass', or something like that; but this time Blair's son was busy eating some dog's mercury and so said nothing. However Grimbart was no longer to be put off.

"Now," he said, "a young chap like you could do worse than to see a bit of the world. At your age I was all over the place and full of spirit. That's the trouble with young badgers today," he went on, "no spirit! I mean to say, what do you do over at your place, your sister and you? 'Ow do you put your time in? That's what I'd like to know. Last night, for instance, what were you doing?"

"Oh, just eating," replied Brock, moving over to another clump of dog's mercury.

"That's just it," said Grimbart triumphantly. "Just eating! What else is there to do 'ere except jus' eating bluebell bulbs and so on. Sometimes I feel as if I was going to turn into a bluebell bulb. That's no way to spend your life!"

"But we weren't eating bluebell bulbs, Mr. Dass," said Blair's son. He coughed modestly. "We were eating potatoes." Grimbart Dass stopped looking at the sky, rolled over and stood up very suddenly.

"Potitoes?" he said.

'Yes, potatoes."

"And where, may I ask, did you get potitoes from?"

"Well," said Brock, "we went down the hill to the new men's houses and we found a great pile of them there and more growing in one of the gardens. We dug them up. They were marvellous."

Grimbart Dass spoke slowly. "You went down the 'ill to the new 'ouses. An' you found some marvellous potitoes; well, well, well . . ."

"Yes, that's what I said, Mr. Dass. We often go down there. Brocka went down there tonight. We . . ."

"Are you both completely and utterly BARMY?" said Grimbart Dass suddenly. " 'Aven't you the sense to know better than to start pinchin' potitoes? 'Aven't you got enough to eat up 'ere on the 'ill? Why can't you stay where you belong, instead of wanderin' all over the country like a couple of thievin' foxes scrumpin' potitoes?"

"But Mr. Dass," said Blair's son, "you were just saying to me . . ."

"Never you mind what I was just saying to you," said Grimbart Dass excitedly. "You just listen to what I'm saying to you now. And what I'm saying to you now is—but just a minute; are you standing there telling me your sister is down there now? 'Ow long 'as she been down there?"

"Well, she's been down there all night, actually."

"All night?" said Grimbart as if he couldn't believe it.

"Yes, Mr. Dass. I wish you wouldn't keep

repeating everything I say."

But Grimbart Dass was already starting down the hill towards the valley.

DAWN came slowly, cloudy and reluctant to the summit of Badger Hill. As it did so Blair and Tasso were making their way slowly back there, tired out and feeling rather gloomy. They moved in file as usual through the woods, Tasso talking and Blair doing a good deal of nodding and agreeing with the clever things Tasso was saying to him. They both seemed quite gloomy to Betsy Blair, who had already returned to First and Last Earth, and was busy putting up piles of leaves and grasses to dry and air for a few days so that she could use them as bedding.

"It is a matter of temperament," Tasso was saying as they approached her through the woods. "He becomes bored."

"Bored with what?" asked Blair.

"Bored with nothing," replied Tasso, "or, on the other hand, to put it another way, with everything."

"I see," said Blair, nodding vigorously, although as a matter of fact he didn't really understand what Tasso could possibly mean. They parted as they reached First and Last Earth, and Tasso, with a bark of greeting to Betsy, went his own way back into his own sett round the other side of the hill.

"Here," said Blair, as he came up to his wife, "let me give you a hand with that."

"No, no, Blair," replied Betsy, who had been ready for this, "I've all but finished."

"No, really," said Blair enthusiastically, "I'll have it done in a jiffy!"

"No, thank you, Blair," replied his wife very firmly.

"Are you sure?"

"Absolutely sure, thank you."

"Oh, well," said Blair, watching her as she expertly piled willowherb and wild thyme, "just as you like." Having failed to get himself involved in this activity, he sighed, sat down, and looked about him.

"Seen Grimbart?" he asked presently.

"No," said Betsy as she passed her husband on the way to the willowherb. "Is there anything wrong with him?"

"He's bored, as a matter of fact," said Blair.

"What on earth do you mean? What's he bored with?" Blair coughed and scratched himself.

"Well, he's bored with nothing; or, to put it in another way, he's bored with everything," Blair replied casually.

"What nonsense you sometimes talk," said his wife, as she passed him again, clouds of fluffy willowherb seeds blowing about her head. "How can he possibly be bored with everything and nothing at the same time?" Blair rose to his feet and thought what a waste of time it was to try to have an intelligent conversation with a woman.

"Anyway," he said rather huffily, "as you don't want me to help you, I think I'll just go and see if he's at home or something." He made his way round the hill towards Grimbart's front door, where he met Lady Grey.

"Hello, there," she said. "Seen Grimbart?" Blair explained that he had come looking for him himself.

"He's bored," he added.

"Really? Thought he seemed a bit out of sorts. What's he bored with?"

Blair considered a moment or two before replying.

"I don't know exactly," he said at last.

"Me neither," said Lady Grey with a laugh, "probably bored with nothing and everything at the same time, don't you think?" But Blair chose not to answer this question.

"Anyway," he said, "I thought I'd see if he wanted a chat or a walk or something."

"Just so," said Lady Grey. And she called into Grimbart's front door with the strange oily, bubbling purr that badgers use to call each other when they are feeling sympathetic. There was no reply so they decided to go inside and look for him. He was not there; however, on their way out they met Tasso coming in.

"He must have gone out for some food," said Tasso slightly uneasily. "He's certainly late getting back. It's quite light outside now."

They sat for a time, thinking of their friend.

"Of course, it's true; there isn't much to do here," said Blair gloomily.

"I suppose this is a dull sort of place," agreed Lady Grey. After a silence they heard another badger approaching them down the tunnel.

"There he is!" said Tasso.

"That must be him!" said Blair.

"At last!" said Lady Grey.

They all stood up to greet the newcomer. But it was only Betsy Blair. They all sat down again, now even more gloomy.

"What on earth is the matter with you all?" said Betsy. Blair sighed.

"It's this place," he said, "it's so dull."

"Poor old Grimbart," said Lady Grey. "I wonder what he's doing?"

"I imagine," said Tasso, "that he is just wandering around. I imagine that he is simply wandering hither and thither, alone, miserable, and weary with life."

"Oh, dear, how sad!" said Betsy quietly.

"Yes," said Lady Grey.

Blair sighed. And so they sat, silent and thoughtful, as they each considered the unhappy Grimbart, who even now might be sleeping fitfully under some thorn bush, or padding dejectedly about the hill and wondering what to do with himself. And so they might have stayed for some long time as everything around them became duller and sadder. But all at once they heard in the silence, the footfall of a badger above them on the forest floor, and they all looked up.

"It must be him," said one of them, almost in a whisper.

"Poor fellow, he must be worn out," said another.

"We must treat him gently," said a third.

"Yes, yes!"

"We will talk to him."

"Cheer him up!"

"Show him that his friends care about him."

There was a thump, a bump, the sound of scuffling feet, and the object of their worry bounded into the hall, galloped round it; stopped; and galloped round again.

"Well," he said triumphantly, "I've got noos for you. While you've been sitting round 'ere enjoying yourselves, I've been busy. Someone 'as to keep their eyes open. An' it's just as well I stayed 'ere last night to keep a watch, just in case. But there's no need to worry. Quite a simple job." Here he paused a moment, turning to Betsy and Blair, and said impressively: "I know where your daughter, Brocka, is."

Blair and Betsy looked at him in astonishment.

"Do you?" said Blair weakly.

"Yes, an' what's more . . ."

"Now, now, my friend," said Tasso soothingly, "come and sit down. You must be very tired. It is, of course, good to hear that you know where Brocka is. Perhaps, after a rest, you will feel like telling us more important news of this kind. We know how you feel. Your friends are here only to help you."

"For 'eavens *sake*," said Grimbart Dass. "I don't need a rest. We've got plans to make!"

"Plans?" said all the others together.

"Year," said Grimbart Dass, "that's what I said. We've got to get 'er out."

"Out?" said the others.

"Well, of course we 'ave. You don't want to leave 'er there do you?" Lady Grey moved over to Grimbart and took him by the shoulders.

"Now then," she said, "just tell us one thing; where is it that we've got to get Brocka out of?"

Grimbart was quiet, and then said slowly:
"She's shut up in a coal 'ouse, down there at
the new houses in the valley."

LADY GREY AT
THE COAL BUNKER

BROCKA, Blair's daughter, had gone down
again into the valley in the best of spirits.
Brock, her brother, had decided not to go
with her that night. She had told him that he
was scared and he had told her that she was
greedy, and they had both been right. It was,
in fact, the thought of those potatoes that had
drawn her on under the fence, and it was only
when she reached the new chicken-wire fence
that ran round Badger Hill that she had
become at all scared herself. But the thought
of the potatoes had drawn her on under the
fence, where it was already bent and broken
by her previous visits, and on into the garden
where they were to be found. Soon she could
smell them. They smelt as delicious as they
had done before. They smelt bitter. They
smelt sweet. They smelt succulent.

But she had hardly begun to eat them
before she smelled something else; a strange

smell; a sweet smell; a wonderful smell. This entrancing new smell she followed like a sleep walker, as it led her down the garden. Soon she found what it was. Brocka knew nothing about raisins—still less about raisins soaked in sherry. She was a simple country girl. When she saw these small brown sweets scattered casually on the soil of the vegetable bed, she did not pause to think what they were or what they were doing there. So far as she was concerned they were simply a new and altogether better kind of potato. She ate them. And every time she found and ate a few, she smelled another few just ahead of her. The more she ate the better they seemed—and the nearer to the house she got. At last, very close to the house, the line of raisins led her up to a large concrete bunker, the trap door of which was held up by a stick. It was dark indeed inside the bunker; but Brocka did not care about that. What she did care about was that from inside she could smell the new, wonderful, irresistible, undeniable smell of raisins soaked in sherry. She pushed past the stick into the coal bunker, and she knocked the stick aside as she passed. When the door slammed shut, catching her back foot as it did so most painfully, she knew that she was trapped.

It was almost dawn when she heard the cautious call of Grimbart Dass, as he nosed about the gardens. Terrified as she had been, with the pain in her back foot and the horror of being caught, as soon as she heard him she let out a loud bark to call him. Lights went on in the house. There was a scuffle as Grimbart retreated, and afterwards the hard footsteps of man coming towards the coal bunker. The lid on the top was lifted, and the frightful, round white face of a man was staring down at her.

The man could see nothing in the darkness of the bunker. Presently, he got a stone and dropped it in. It fell right on poor Brocka's back, and she yelped like a dog. The man, who no doubt got a scare himself, slammed down the lid and went away.

The silence of her new prison fell again, and with it darkness. Hours later there were chinks of daylight to be seen through cracks at the doors of the bunker. Hours later again there was more noise; the noise of men's steps and men's talk; the noise of grinding and banging all round the bunker. Suddenly the trap-door of the bunker was lifted, and in its place was thrust an old piece of garden railing that fitted tight into the slots of the trap. Through the bars of this railing some potato and stale bread was thrust. Later, and from time to time, men's children came to look at Brocka, gazing through the bars into the darkness of the bunker at the back of which Brocka cowered, back pressed to the wall, and ready to bite. Once a stick was poked through at her, pushing into her ribs. She bit at it, cutting the end to ribbons, and it was withdrawn and admired by the men.

As darkness of night came again she was alone. Miserable, hungry and dead tired, she moved over to the bars of the railing, pushing her way past the food that she would not touch. She tried the bars in her teeth time after time, but they were too strong for her. She pushed her soft nose out between them and smelled longingly at the night airs that drifted about the garden. A wonderful damp mist lay about that seemed to have been drawn down from the woods of her beloved home. It was very quiet. She moved back into her prison and licked at her hurt foot which was sore.

All at once there was a click from a milk bottle beside the house, followed by another, and then by the rolling and clashing of a number of them as they toppled from their places beside the back door. She was terrified at this new disturbance too—until, with joy, she heard a well-known voice whispering angrily beside the coal-bunker:

"For 'eavens *sake*; must you move about like a railway train? You'll 'ave the whole lot of us in trouble if you can't keep a bit quiet!"

There followed more chinking and rolling of bottles accompanied by scuffling sounds, and the noise of her father saying:

"Frightfully sorry! I just didn't quite realise; these cursed things seem to be everywhere!" as the latter picked himself up from among the milk bottles he had scattered and which in turn had scattered him.

But Grimbart was already examining the bars of the railing that formed the gate to Brocka's prison, while Brocka licked him enthusiastically on the nose.

"Don't worry," he whispered. "We'll 'ave

you out of 'ere in just a jiffy."

Brocka sensibly kept quiet and watched eagerly. But Grimbart had been wrong about how easy it was to deal with those bars. He scraped the base with his claws. He tried to push up the gate with his nose. Finally he took the bars in his jaws and tried to bend them. But it was no good. On the top of the bunker was the lid, which might have been raised indeed in a jiffy, but for the one matter that prevented it. Badgers can run, bite and dig; but they cannot jump. Grimbart sat back and sighed.

"Potitoes!" he said bitterly; at which Brocka did feel rather ashamed of herself.

"Just a minute," said her father. He scuttled off into the blackness of the garden, carefully avoiding milk bottles, and returned in a short time with another badger.

"Good evening, Lady Grey," said Brocka rather miserably when she saw who it was.

"Evenin'," replied the latter. "Now then, stand aside!" And, placing herself squarely in front of the bars, she bent her fine head and gripped the railing in her jaws. Then she shut her eyes and pulled. She pulled until her paws seemed to flatten into the ground and the muscles on her shoulders stood out with the strain. And as she pulled the bar bent. Then she stopped and pulled the bar next to it the other way, until it seemed that her whole skull would crack with the effort. But as she pulled that bar bent too. Then she stood back. Brocka was not a very large badger, being young. And she simply walked out between those bars as though they had been a gateway.

"Oh, thank you, thank you! . . ." began Brocka. But at that moment there was from the other side of the house a rapid:

"Ark. . .ark. . .ark" of a badger warning call.

"That's Tasso," Grimbart said simply. "Let's go." And as Brocka heard once more the hard step of a man's boot on the concrete path the badgers were off with a ringing clash of milk bottles and a rather rude curse from Lady Grey, so that by the time the man's footfall had reached the concrete coal bunker the whole garden was as peaceful and quiet as it had ever been. The man switched on a torch that shone weakly yellow in the misty night, and directed it on the milk bottles as they lay higgledy-piggledy about the path. He picked them up and set them to rights. Then he went over to the bunker and shone the beam upon the railing just where it was bent in a neat curve. He looked at it for a few moments in astonishment, and then gazed into the darkness up towards the woods that rose at the end of his garden. They could only be seen by the dim line where their blackness met the dim sky, which curved up to the very summit of Badger Hill and then down again.

"Well, would you believe it!" he said.

TASSO woke up one morning, and leaving his warm bedchamber where his beloved Eleanor Grey lay sleeping, made his way drowsily down the step at the bedchamber door. This step had been thoughtfully provided as a good place to defend themselves from in case of need, as is the custom with badgers. He made his way along the tunnel to the outside world. The entrance to the sett was sealed up with old bracken against the cold, and this he had to push through to get out. It was a bright morning, made brighter since during the night it had snowed again.

Because it was winter. As the months had passed and the festivals of Michaelmas and Martinmas came round, so they were kept with less and less enthusiasm by the five badgers of First and Last Earth. As the leaves fell from the trees, and as the very snails withdrew into companies under stones and in hollows and sealed their shells against the cold, so the badgers found it harder and harder to stay awake for any long time.

By the time Childermas came round at midwinter, it was all they could do to celebrate at all; and after a sleepy excursion to the edge of the woods, they one by one yawned, made excuses to each other, and ambled back to their respective homes to plug their doors up with branches and retire thankfully to warm beds of dry leaves. They went out now each on their own as the mood took them for a little food and a bit of a stroll. They troubled each other but little; for each understood the needs of his neighbour as he understood the need he felt himself, for the long rest and contented loneliness of the secret time of the year. For winter is the secret time when bluebell shoots push through the soil unseen and buds form and grow on empty boughs. It is the time when insects are wrapped secretly in silk and small animals dream silently, hidden among dead leaves; when the earth grows hard and secretive with frost, and the life of puddles and ponds is hidden under delicate covers of ice.

Tasso blinked in the brightness of the snow.

For inches round his doorway, and round the other doorways of First and Last Earth, the heat from the homes had melted the snow altogether, and from each doorway a thin column of steam rose into the cold, still air. But the sun had some warmth to offer—its special, mild, prickly warmth that it gives in winter, and that fills one with longing to be out and stretch one's legs a little. As Tasso padded down the path from his sett into the forest, he was not the only creature to be abroad. As he walked over moss that seemed to glow with queerly bright greenness, he pushed past green ivy, and insects tempted out by the sun fell drunkenly from the nectar of the flowers they had fed upon; and he heard the scream of a vixen fox as she moved somewhere far away among trees. After he had gone, and as the steam rose steadily from the doorways of the First and Last Earth a little wren appeared among the bushes, bobbing and singing—but then disappeared like a mouse as it heard other noise.

It was the noise of children from the valley, running and shouting through the frozen woods, scraping up balls of thin, wet snow to throw at each other and at trees, and kicking at the fungi that grew like shells around old roots.

They came helter-skelter up the hill, forcing their way through old brambles and brown bracken, for they were determined to get to the very summit of Badger Hill. When they got there they stopped short in surprise, for they had seen the three columns of steam that rose from the ground mysteriously into the sunlight. At first they were afraid of them but eventually one crept forward to examine this curiosity, and when nothing had happened to him he was joined by his friends. They smelled at the steam as it rose oddly out of the bracken-filled hole, and they said:

"Cor! Stinks!"

Then one of them noticed something on the ground where the snow had melted from the edge of the hole, and picked it up quickly before the others saw it. The three crowded together to examine it.

"It's a dagger," said one.

"It looks like a Roman dagger, or something."

They each looked at it, snatching it from

each other, and turning over the thing that Grimbart Dass had thrown out of his sett in the autumn and had forgotten all about. It was a great find. Still chattering the children turned about and left to make their way back home towards lunch. They agreed to ask their fathers about it.

Blair Badger turned in his sleep, as he dreamed that one hundred men with two hundred ferocious dogs were storming over the summit of First and Last Earth above him, but that the dogs were barking like children for some reason that he couldn't understand. Then suddenly he was awake. He got up and shook himself. Surely he had heard something? Or was it only part of his dream that seemed to echo in his head? He scratched himself and ambled down the tunnel to his front door. Pushing aside the bracken, he stepped out rather cautiously into the glittering morning. There was, he thought, a smell of men about. Carefully he stepped out into the snow that was melting fast now. Then he stopped. He could smell and see the tracks of men, and, such as they were they seemed to lead right across the summit of the hill and to reach Grimbart Dass's front door. In the wet melting of the morning they were disappearing fast, yet Blair felt sure he was right. Suddenly overcome with fright he bolted right inside Grimbart's sett with much bumping and noise and some warning barks that he uttered in spite of himself almost; and with some relief he heard the master of the house thumping down towards his hall from the bedchamber. Grimbart appeared yawning.

"For 'eavens sake," he said sleepily, "what's goin' on?"

"I just came in," said Blair, "to see if you were all right."

Grimbart stopped yawning and looked at him.

"Well," he said slowly, "it's very kind of you to worry about me, of course. As it 'appens I was asleep until you came in and woke me up."

"Oh, good!" said Blair.

"Yes," said Grimbart. "It was good."

"You see I thought there were men about outside." Grimbart eyed Blair gloomily.

"Well, then," he said, "let's go and have a look, shall we?"

Tasso meanwhile had enjoyed his morning ramble. He galloped happily among the woods, pulling at red hips and haws, spindleberry and snowberry, and returned in high spirits to First and Last Earth where he was surprised to find Grimbart and Blair standing outside Grimbart's front door.

"I'm sure there were tracks here," Blair was saying as though he wasn't at all sure, and as he nosed about at the wet ground from which snow and smell had both vanished.

"*Buon giorno a tutti*," said Tasso cheerfully as he came up.

"Ah, Tasso," said Grimbart. "Have you been out long?"

"No, no. I have only been down to the stream and back. It is a morning of great beauty."

"Yes," said Grimbart Dass. "And did you notice anything *odd* when you came out? Anything like, for example, some tracks of men?"

Tasso looked astonished.

"No, no, no," he said, "not a thing. There was snow about and it hadn't been moved across since it fell. But what's this all about?"

a sure there were tracks here," Blair was saying.

"Oh, nothing," said Grimbart, gazing at the crest-fallen Blair. "It's just that Blair 'ere was dreaming about some dogs that barked like children, and so 'e very kindly decided to come and wake me up to find out if I was all right."

"Really?" said Tasso, looking in surprise at poor Blair.

"Yes," said Grimbart, "and if it's all right with you I think I'll be getting back to bed."

The sky darkened suddenly as low, heavy cloud passed across the sun. Tasso shivered.

"Well," he said, "I think I'll be off back to bed too. Cheerio!"

"Cheerio!" said Blair sadly. He wandered over First and Last Earth, swinging his head back and forth in a puzzled fashion until he got back to his own front door.

"What a silly fool I am!" he said sadly to himself. And he made his way down, stopping only to push back the branches across his door as the snow began to fall again, this time more determinedly. When night fell it was still snowing, and the wind rose and sighed among the trees and blew the snow over the ground in a freezing dust. It piled up the dust into all kinds of strange shapes on the bumps and hollows of Badger Hill, from which all signs of life had vanished into winter secrecy again. In the warm comfort of his bedchamber Blair turned over.

"I'm sure there was something," he said. And deep in untidy bracken in his bedchamber Grimbart Dass also turned over.

"Dogs barkin' like children," he said, "or was it children barkin' like dogs?"

So the night passed and a short grey day followed. Snow melted and fell again; winds blew, singing through the branches of the fir trees and clattering through the branches of elms. Rains came with the wind and battered and drummed on the windows of the new houses in the valley, inside one of which the dagger was taken out and shown round again and again. There was talk there, too, as the long winter passed, of the loss of potatoes so carefully grown, of bent railing and of smashed chicken wire fence, so expensively erected. One day the dagger, carefully wrapped in newspaper, was taken on a bus into Canterbury itself, and was carried through the narrow, muddy streets that bustled with people and motor cars, past the bright electric lights of shops and past the great stone gateway of Canterbury Cathedral that rose above everything else and disappeared in the mists of the early winter evening. So the dagger was carried into a narrow lane and up some stairs and into a room. There it was taken from its newspaper and examined by experts. And some said it was Romano-British, and others said it was Gallico-Roman; while yet others considered that it was Saxon with influence of Viking, Celtic and other, earlier periods. But all agreed that it was probably—although by no means certainly—very old; unless indeed it was not so old as they thought it probably was. And all agreed that it was not very well preserved, and of 'purely antiquarian interest', which meant that they weren't quite sure what it was, but, being experts, didn't like to say so.

Through all these and other activities of men, the badgers of First and Last Earth peacefully passed the secret season with yawns, snores, dreams, and short excursions through dripping woods under brilliant winter stars. Like the sensible animals they were, they never worried much about the past or the future. The present was the important thing, and that was restful, comfortable, and pleasant enough.

PLANS OF WAR

GRIMBART Dass lay asleep in his untidy bedchamber. He lay curled up, sucking mouthfuls of slack tummy, making a rather wet sucking noise as he did so. However, there was no one to hear this, so it didn't matter.

But suddenly he was awake. He turned over and tried to go back to sleep again. But he couldn't. He was very awake indeed. He was feeling things, and feeling them extremely. First of all he was feeling like going out. And second he was feeling really hungry. He rose to his feet, among bracken, and then sat down again blinking. His bedchamber that for so long had seemed the best place in the world, now looked old, frowsty and sad. He jumped up and raced along the tunnel to his hall. This place, too, which had seemed so comfortable and cosy, and even at times, elegant, now appeared gloomy and messy with bits of last year's leaves scattered about it. At the doorway to the sett he pushed impatiently through the bracken that closed it up, thrusting his long nose out into the evening. He moved his nose in figures of eight, and snuffled deeply at the wonderful airs that blew past the doorway. It was a windy evening in the mad month of March. The airs passed into Grimbart's nose like electricity, and made him shiver with excitement. They told him of many things—of the flowering of dog's mercury outside in the woods; of the nearness of baby voles and moles; of the flowers on the bare boughs of ash and alder; of the gathering of hordes of toads for ancient rituals in a pond, to reach which they would hop all night; of the beginning in general of the season of spring.

Grimbart gave a sudden bark, jumped outside into the evening, and ambled cheerfully round the First and Last Earth. No-one seemed to be about, and he had begun to make his way down to the stream, when a doorway in the Earth caught the attention of his delicate nose. He pushed into it and sniffed a smell that he had not smelled for several years, and that he could not even quite remember. But he was soon reminded when the large shape of Lady Grey appeared rather suddenly within the tunnel.

"Yes?" said her ladyship coldly.

"Oh, good evening," said the curious Grimbart. "I was just passing and I thought I noticed . . ."

"You did," said the other.

"You mean to say? . . ." said Grimbart.

"Babies; three for me and two for Betsy."

"Well, I'll be blowed!" said Grimbart excitedly.

"Yes," said Lady Grey, "and now you can clear off!"

"Oh, yes," replied Grimbart hastily, as he remembered also the short tempers of badger mothers, "naturally; well, congratulations and so on, an' all the best."

"Thank you," said Lady Grey.

"Well, I'll be off, then."

"Goodbye," said her ladyship.

Grimbart turned and ambled off, looking back only once to the tunnel mouth, where he could see the formidable mother-of-three still watching him to make sure he *was* off.

He gave a chuckle and set off into the woods

where he soon picked up the trail of Tasso and Blair who were ahead of him. He went after them, kicking his heels, and stopping to investigate small smells on the way; and he was quite a way away by the time the tramp of men's feet was heard coming up the hill towards First and Last Earth through the twilight.

There were two men and a child. They reached the summit of the hill and walked round it. They looked into the tunnels of the setts, bending down to gaze into them, although they could see no further than the first few feet; for after that the tunnels had a sharp turn in them to keep their secrets from prying eyes. The child went over to the tunnel beside which he had found the dagger, and pointed to the place. The three of them nodded and talked. As darkness came down they turned away, and set off back towards the valley, and silence fell again at First and Last Earth.

Grimbart Dass meanwhile had caught up with his two friends Tasso and Blair. These two were at a loose end, as badger fathers tend to be when there are babies at home, and joined by Grimbart, they dashed across the country in their old way, across fields where in fading light peewits tumbled and cried their names wildly, while in the bare thickets of the hedges the blackbird sang. They saw two hares fighting in a field watched solemnly by their women folk; and these were so intent upon their boxing match that only when the badgers went right up to them and shouted did they give up and race away. Coming to a stream, the badgers waded in and bathed, swam across to the other side and stood there in the running water, sluicing it with their front paws over their faces. When they turned for home they were tired but in good spirits, and made their way through the bracken of the woods with shouts and snorts and occasional long-drawn screams of happiness that rang among the empty trees and echoed down the hill.

They went careless of everything, until as they came over the edge of an old gravel pit, there was a growl from the blackness below.

The three of them stopped short and smelled into the darkness of the pit. There was a rustle and a whisper of feet—and no distance away in the darkness of the pit stood two dogs from the valley houses, out for a run and very excited. For a few moments the two groups of animals stared at each other with mouths shut, very surprised. At last, one of the dogs advanced, teeth bared and growling low, all ready for a bit of a brawl.

Grimbart was in front, as it happened. He lowered his head, as if he was asking the dog to grab the back of his neck—and all at once everything happened very quickly. As the dog jumped to grab that neck, and its teeth closed on Grimbart's fur, Grimbart brought his head up with jaws open and grabbed the dog by the throat, pulling back as he did so; and the dog, with a yelp, was thrown into the air to fall with a yelp on its back. Tasso and Blair meanwhile seemed suddenly to have grown enormous. With their grey fur fluffed up they looked twice as big as they were, and they waddled very low on the ground down into the pit towards the other dog with growls and snarls that made them look and sound like ferocious engines of some kind.

The brawl was over. The two dogs ran off in opposite directions, while Grimbart shook himself and cursed them as they went. The brawl was over and easily enough won. But the three badgers were not in quite such good spirits as they had been. Badgers are well able to defend themselves, but fighting is no pleasure to them. They made their way back towards First and Last Earth along ditches and through thickets, with Grimbart feeling rather chilly on the back of his neck where the dog had torn out some fur.

"Anyway," said Tasso, "it is good that they were not too close to the Earth."

"And we gave them a jolly good scare," said Blair.

"Yes," said Grimbart. "It should keep them away for a bit."

But as they drew near to home they stopped short yet again; for they smelled the now familiar and fearful smell of man. It seemed to be everywhere round the Earth, and right up to the doorways of the setts, as though these had been examined, and the smells were still quite strong. The men had been there only a short time ago.

As light gathered and filtered down into the woods the next morning, the badgers of the

First and Last Earth were together again in the hall of Blair's sett.

"I kept tellin' you we ought to have moved," Grimbart was saying. "This is only the beginning. They'll be everywhere before you know where you are."

"But we can't move far now," wailed Betsy Blair, "the babies are too small."

"Don't you worry," said Lady Grey grimly to Betsy. "I would just like to see any creature tryin' to get hold of our babies."

"There's nothing for it," said Blair. "There's no answer to it. We're for it," he added miserably.

"One moment, please!" said Tasso, and the others looked at him. "We badgers," he said, "live on this hill as other badgers before us have lived for countless years gone by. And live here we will!"

"Yes," said Grimbart, "that's all very well. But what if men come to finish us off?"

"Men," said Tasso, "live by day and above the ground. We badgers live by night and below the ground."

"You don't say!" observed Grimbart Dass.

"So," continued Tasso, as though his

friend had not spoken, "if the men choose to attack us we must be ready for them in our own way. We must meet them badger-fashion! We must show them that we do not intend that victory shall be theirs! We must be everywhere and nowhere at the same time! We must fight tooth and claw with courage and cunning for this place which is our home—until men know that it is ours—or perish in the attempt!"

Lady Grey snorted. "How?" she said.

"How?" repeated Tasso.

"Yes, 'ow?" said Grimbart.

Tasso looked hurt. "Naturally," he said, "if you will allow me without continual interruption, I will tell you."

When Tasso had finished his plans the badgers talked among themselves for a time, and then went off to their various homes, bidding one another goodrest. In their various beds they each thought over sleepily the clever things that Tasso had said to them. 'Underground warfare', said Grimbart to himself, as he yawned. 'Guerrilla tactics', whispered Betsy Blair, as she settled into the fresh green bracken. 'Organisation is everythin',' murmured Lady Grey as her cubs squirmed about her. 'Diversity is unity', said Blair Badger sleepily, 'or was it unity is diversity?'.

During the nights that followed there were various quiet activities in various parts of Badger Hill. There was digging. There was moving of bedding. There were muttered discussions in thickets where new sandy caverns had appeared. And one night a large brown sow badger and a small grey sow badger might have been seen carrying small wriggling creatures with new sharp teeth and newly opened eyes like elderberries. They might have been seen, that is, if there had been anybody there to see them, which there wasn't; and if there had been any light to see by, which there wasn't either. The large sow badger carried three of these wriggling creatures, who mewed like doves, one at a time, to one cavern. And the small sow badger carried two mewing wrigglers one at a time to another place.

So the nights on Badger Hill passed quietly, and the days passed also quietly.

THE BATTLE OF
BADGER HILL

THE men and the dogs came up the hill without warning one beautiful morning in May. There were five men and three dogs, and the men carried spades and the dogs ran beside them. They were all quiet for they had a hard and exciting day ahead of them. They pushed through bluebells that flowered in dense clouds of blue among the trees, and they pushed through the uncurling green of bracken and bramble. They were going to find out about the summit of Badger Hill. They hoped to find some interesting things there, such as ancient daggers and lively badgers. Although none of them knew much about either of these, they felt sure they were going to have a good time anyway.

It was wonderfully quiet up on the summit. While the men put down their spades and admired the view across the city where the towers of the Cathedral rose, the dogs raced around sniffing and barking at the holes in the hill.

"We'll take it easy," said one of the men. "There's no need to rush it."

The men began to fill up the holes. They blocked them thoroughly with chalk and earth and banged down their spades on them to make sure about it. The sun rose into the sky as they worked, and all went well for a time, until suddenly something happened. One of the dogs found a tunnel higher up on the summit that was hidden by bracken—an old hole of some kind—and the dog began to bark furiously.

"Look at that," said one of the men, "she's on to something."

And he walked over to catch his dog, calling; but the dog would wait no longer, and by the time the men ran up shouting the dog had disappeared into the hole. As the men gazed into the tunnel there was pandemonium inside it. There was barking and growling, yapping and a yelping; and it all echoed from inside the hill in a strange and frightful way.

The men rushed for their spades and began to dig. They had to dig through hard earth and harder chalk, and what with the echoing noise of the dog and whatever it had found they dug all the harder until their arms began to ache and the sweat ran down their faces. Then their spades struck the stone.

It was no use. They had to dig all round the stone to dislodge it. It took five of them twenty minutes of hard digging. When they finally pulled aside the stone they found they were looking into a stone chamber that had nothing in it but their dog, who was bleeding from a torn ear, and who was barking furiously at a hole in the far side of the chamber that she was too frightened to go down. Rather wearily the men put down their spades and pulled off their dog; but that was just the beginning. The two other dogs had so far been made to sit by their owners, until one of them now saw something that he could not resist following. It was a grey shape that had appeared suddenly from among the brambles lower down where a little stream ran out of the hill. It was all too obvious as it crashed away through the undergrowth, and all too much for the dog. The grey shape zig-zagged off at great speed, and was pursued by the dog into the distance.

The men cursed and put the other two dogs on a leash. They had forgotten all about daggers by now. They wanted badgers. They filled up the two newly discovered holes and took the dogs over to a third, which they made sure was the only one left. They spaced out round the hill-top, put a dog into the hole, took up their spades, and waited. At first all was quiet. Then the fight began underground, and they felt sure of getting one badger. As soon as the noise was heard the men began to dig again above the place where the noise was coming from. They dug fast and furious, for they judged it was quite deep underground. They dug two or three feet of sand, earth and chalk in no time, but then the noise moved away from them and began at another point in the earth. The men cursed and ran to this new place. The sweat was pouring from them by now, but they dug again with a will. As they got nearer to the fight they had to go carefully with their spades for they might have struck through to their dog.

"We've got him this time!" shouted one of them as he felt his spade fall through into the tunnel. But the noise moved again deeper underground. From there there was noise for a time that rose to a sudden wild yelping and growling—and then there was silence.

The men leaned on their spades in the heat of the day. They called and panted. They moved round the summit. There was nothing. They spent the afternoon calling and looking, digging at holes and cursing. There were no daggers to be found. With their third dog still on the leash they set out at last to look for the dog that had bolted after the grey shape earlier in the day. It turned up at last, weary and wanting to be carried. They found it at another hole at the far side of the hill, half a mile away.

"Well," said one of the men, "seems we've lost one dog and killed two badgers. Maybe that's the lot of them done for, and good riddance!"

They turned for home as darkness fell, five tired men and two tired dogs. They walked down the hill among the darkening trees. They talked, and as they talked they convinced themselves that they had cleared the woods of badgers; for these men knew as little about badgers—perhaps less—than the badgers knew about them, and that, we might say, was lucky for the badgers. It was as they came to the edge of the woods that they saw it. It was a great, brown creature with fluffed up fur, that in the vagueness of the dusk looked the size of a small bear.

The dogs, tired as they were, advanced and began to harry this monster. But the monster fought back. It ran about, back and forth with the dogs madly after it. It rushed among the men, biting and snarling, and spades thumped down and fell behind it, and dogs ran in mad tiredness among shouting. It passed so close to one of the men that it ran over his foot, and tore the leather clean from the top of his boot as it passed. Then the noise went underground again, and though the men shouted until they were hoarse, they could not get the dogs out. At last the dogs reappeared, one dragging a badly bitten foot and the other one cut through the flank. The men were glad to see them at all, and examined their wounds as the dogs tried to wag their tails.

It had been a hard day, but so far as the men

were concerned a victorious one—so at least they convinced themselves. They reckoned that they might have cleared out the badgers altogether with a bit of luck.

"Just as well, too," said one of them as they climbed the fence in the darkness and made their way down to the road. "Those things are a menace."

"It's not safe for the children with those things about."

"That last one bit clean through my boots."

"They're vermin, that's what they are."

Their voices died away from the woods. A gentle wind rose, singing through the fir trees of the plantation, and whispering through the new leaves of beeches and oaks, alders and chestnuts. It blew through the silent night, and blew away the night altogether as the sun came up over the downs. In the valley five men slept in late that morning, and two brave dogs, bandaged and ill, also slept, twitching sometimes and whimpering in their sleep. The day passed and the wind blew clouds across the sky. It was very quiet on Badger Hill. The clouds hid stars and moon and the darkness was as deep as the silence. Even on the summit there was no noise except for the whispering feet of mice and the occasional wingflap of a restless bird.

But at last there was something. A black nose appeared from a sandy hole somewhere in a thicket. It appeared cautiously and waved in figures of eight. The nose was followed by a long black and white head and a grey body. Blair Badger turned and spoke into the tunnel.

"Come," he said, "there is no danger."

Then he set off into the woods. In a short time the nose of Betsy Blair appeared also at the sandy mouth of the tunnel. She, too, came out, and turning, gave a soft, oily, bubbling purr into the tunnel. From inside it a mewing noise like a dove was heard, and in a moment two tiny badgers with elderberry eyes tumbled out excitedly, falling over things and getting in their own way. Far away, meanwhile, from an imposing entrance of Grey Hatch, another nose appeared, followed by a large brown one, followed by three very small noses that mewed like doves, or chattered like squirrels for something to eat.

Only at the very summit of the hill was there

still silence. Brock and Brocka were out together that night, and wandered to the summit in search of food. They drank together in the stream that ran out of the side of the hill; but there was no noise except for the noise they made themselves. After a time they left again, and the silence went on until it was dawn. As the sun rose in a cleared sky and shot gold beams among the alder and chestnut thickets, Grimbart Dass came out of the side of the hill. He had thought that he was dead as he lay in First and Last Earth.

"I'm dead", he said to himself. "Dead as last year's leaves; dead as old stones and bones; dead as the dog in the bedchamber."

But he was not dead, although the dog he had fought and who had fought him right up to the door of his own bedchamber—where Grimbart had turned as he stood upon the step at the door and used his terrible teeth in a long grip—was dead. Grimbart Dass was hurt, but he was not dead. He was badly hurt, and he moved slowly down the stream and took a long drink. As the light strengthened, he climbed wearily to the very top of the hill, going slowly, just above where the great stone of the chamber had been dug out by the men, and he gazed shortsightedly out into the morning. He was definitely not dead.

"Well, well, well," he said quietly; "surprise, surprise!"

12

GRIMBART DASS

WEEKS later the nightjar was back in the night-woods, and rattled cheerfully as he flew after moths and flies that he was collecting for his babies who waited impatiently for him in their dark nest. Stars glittered down among the trees that were blown by summer breezes, and so rocked the twiggy nests of wood-pigeons and rooks, as though these were so many boats bobbing on a calm sea.

Brock and Brocka were far from their home, and wandering at the very edge of the fir plantation where their father's old sett had been, and where they themselves had been babies. They pushed under the fence there, and Brocka paused to eat up a slug, while Brock made his way dreamily down through the pasture towards the stream, along the old path that he had first taken as a tiny creature a year before. He was, in fact, one year old and a bit, and he was a well-grown young badger, fit and ready for anything. He walked down the hill, among feathery cow parsley and thistles that had suddenly grown up taller than himself, in a sort of dreamy swagger, and he muttered to himself as he went.

"With a savage growl," Brock was saying to himself, "the enormous dog hurled itself at the young badger, and gripped the brave creature in its fangs. But, quick as a flash . . ."

At this point Brock noticed a large beetle crawling hastily into the undergrowth. He stopped, licked it up, and chewed it wetly.

"Quick as a flash," he continued, "the badger turned and flung the dog aside with a careless laugh. Yet the cowardly fiend had not had enough punishment. With unbelievable strength it returned to the attack, where the noble badger waited to meet it. Quick as a flash . . ."

Brock paused as he realised that something was coming down the hill behind him. It was quite a large something. Brock forgot all about the brave young badger immediately, and began to feel a bit frightened. It might have been a dog, and it might have been many things; but most of all it seemed like another badger—perhaps some unfriendly creature that had claimed this bit of country for itself, and would be all ready to teach Brock a lesson for setting foot in it. Brock looked at the stream and the steep railway embankment beyond it. Running away seemed rather difficult. He got quietly down to the stream, pushed into the tall flowering yellow iris there, shut his eyes, and waited as his feet got wetter and wetter. It seemed that, with a bit of luck, he might not be noticed by whatever it was, and could just wait for it to get past; and so escape with nothing worse than wet feet. He was just beginning to forget about the other creature and concentrate on the frightful coldness of his feet, when there was the noise of splashing and of rushes being pushed aside, and Brock realised that the creature was coming straight for him.

With a brave scream and closed eyes Brock rushed suddenly from his hiding place at top speed and with such force that he knocked the other creature off its feet and into the water, where it struggled among water and weed with a great deal of muddy splashing. Brock had opened his eyes in surprise, but rather quickly decided that now was the time to make a run for it, and disappeared as fast as his legs would carry him up into the pasture.

Brocka, meanwhile, was wondering where her brother had got to, and was making her way along the bank of the stream, when she saw a badger covered with weed and mud making *its* way, coughing, to the bank. Brocka, who although she was very fond of her brother, had no great opinion of his good sense, immediately decided that she knew what had happened.

"What on earth are you doing falling about in the stream? Can't you watch where you're going?" she said. But to Brocka's surprise, the badger brushed some weed from its face, and answered in a voice that was not her brother's, but which was very well known to her in spite of being rather watery.

"Very funny," it said, "extremely laughable; what a good joke! Oh, ah, ha!"

"Good gracious me," said Brocka. "Mr. Dass! I'm terribly sorry. I thought my brother Brock was here somewhere. But what are you doing falling into the water?" Grimbart Dass scraped a blob of mud from his chest.

I knocked the other creature into the water..

"In point of fact," he said, "I didn't fall into the water."

"Didn't you?" said Brocka. She found this a little hard to believe as Grimbart Dass stood dripping in front of her, but she liked Grimbart Dass and felt that it would be impolite to disagree with him.

"No," said Grimbart Dass firmly. "I didn't".

"Well, of course, if you say so," said Brocka, "it's just that as I saw you coming out of the stream all wet and muddy, I thought perhaps that something like that must have happened, but if you say so I expect there must be some other reason."

"Well, of course I was in the water. But in point of fact I didn't fall into it. In point of fact I was shuvved in!"

"Shoved in?" said Brocka.

"Year, *shuvved* in. I was just walking into the stream to set off on my travels again without botherin' anybody or makin' any fuss, when I was shuvved in very 'ard from behind!"

"But good gracious, who would want to do a thing like that?" asked Brocka in astonishment.

"Year," said Grimbart Dass, spitting out a last bit of weed, "that's a very good question, and one that I was already wonderin' about myself, as it 'appens. You say your brother was round 'ere somewhere?"

"Well, yes," replied Brocka, "but why should he want to push you into the stream?"

"I wouldn't know," replied Grimbart. "You see, no one told me anything about it at all. No one come up and said, 'Now Grimbart, old chap, I'm going to push you into the stream for a bit of a lark and because I like the noise it makes!' 'Ooever it was just came up and shuvved, and after that they 'opped it. 'Ooever it was didn't wait about to say, 'sorry about that—I just like pushing badgers into streams,' or anything like that; they just shuvved and 'opped it. No question of 'do you mind?' or 'by your leave', or 'excuse me', or anything like that. Just shuv and off!"

Grimbart Dass might have spoken further on this subject, but Brocka suddenly realised the importance of something he had said to her before.

"But surely," she said, "you're not leaving

us, Mr. Dass?"

Grimbart looked up.

"Year," he said, "I thought it was time I was off again. There's nothing here for me really, you know, Brocka. I'm not important around 'ere. I'm just the sort of creature that when someone sees 'im, they say to themselves: 'Oh, there's old Grimbart! Let's 'ave a bit of a laugh and push 'im into a stream!' "

Grimbart shivered a bit and shook himself.

"But don't be silly, Mr. Dass," said Brocka, "we're all very fond of you here. Everyone knows what a brave and clever creature you are!"

Grimbart looked up again and began to feel a little better.

"Do they?" he said.

"Of course they do," said Brocka. "Why, you're the hero of Badger Hill!"

"I am?" said Grimbart Dass.

"Well, naturally," said Brocka. "Everyone knows how you fought with that dog at First and Last Earth!"

"It was two dogs, actually," said Grimbart Dass, who was suddenly feeling much better. "It may even have been three or four. I couldn't tell in the dark. Anyway, it felt like three or four. But, as I say, there's nothing for me here now. The best thing for me is, well, travel; up stumps; make a clean break with the past; turn over a new leaf; and so on."

"But you won't be any less lonely travelling by yourself," said Brocka, "and we all get lonely. I get lonely too, sometimes."

"Do you?" said Grimbart Dass.

"Of course I do. I often see no one but Brock for days at a time."

"Yes," said Grimbart thoughtfully. "I can imagine that that could be a bit trying. I suppose," he added, "he doesn't spend all his time pushing badgers into streams, does 'e?"

"No," said Brocka firmly.

"No, no," said Grimbart Dass; "silly thought really. I just wondered. Still, if I might give you a little advice I can't 'elp feeling that, when you're out with your brother—stay clear of streams! Give 'em a wide berth! Just a piece of advice, of course."

Brocka and Grimbart were by this time wandering along the bank of the stream, and in all this conversation Grimbart forgot about his resolve to set off into the world again. He had just remembered it, however, and was about to say something like: 'Farewell, Brocka! Remember me to the others, and tell them that wherever I am I shall remember them!'—when he heard a humming noise in the side of the bank of the stream among some old roots. Brocka heard it too, and they both knew what it was.

"Wasps," said Brocka.

"Year," said Grimbart.

And without further ado they set to. They were wrong, for it wasn't wasps but honey bees that had escaped and set up home in the wild, but that didn't worry the two badgers. They pulled the bark from the roots, and sleepy bees in thousands woke up and swarmed all about them buzzing and trying to sting. The badgers ate everything—bees, grubs and honey, and the air was so full of the noises of furious buzzing and enthusiastic eating, that it was only as they finished and sat back, that they heard the cautious sounds of something approaching them. It seemed in fact to be several things, and the things were being awfully quiet. They were coming along the bank of the stream. Grimbart said very quietly to Brocka:

"Up the bank!"

She went up silently, and Grimbart followed her and waited at the top in silence, ready to deal with these quiet stalkers, whoever they might be.

The first of them was just a bite away from Grimbart's ready teeth, when a twig snapped somewhere, and the leader of the stalkers turned round to whisper loudly:

"For heaven's sake Blair; silence!"

And Grimbart gave up all thoughts of biting and said in surprise:

"Lady Grey; what a shock you just gave us!"

This remark from just above Lady Grey's head, in fact gave her even more of a shock, and she fell back with a bark, thus pushing Blair, who was just behind her, off his feet, and who in turn bowled over Tasso, who fell on top of Brock, causing him to yelp.

"Silence!" said Lady Grey sterny, and as her companions picked themselves up, she directed her attention to the head above her. "Grimbart," she whispered urgently, "thank heavens you're here! And what are you doing soaking wet? But never mind that now. Have you seen it?"

"Seen what?"

"Earlier this evening," whispered Lady Grey hoarsely, Brock saw some creature or other down here. He says it was extremely fierce, and enormously large. Luckily, Brock fought most bravely with it and managed to push it into the stream so that he could escape and get help!"

Grimbart Dass looked at them for a moment. "Year," he said slowly; "that was lucky; it was very lucky and very brave, too. Perhaps," he said as he ambled down the bank and up to Brock, "you would just show me 'ow it happened. I imagine that you was standing about 'ere fighting with this monster, and the monster was standing about 'ere. Is that 'ow it was?"

"Yes, Mr. Dass, said Brock. "It was a frightful-looking creature."

"I see," went on Grimbart, nodding thoughtfully, "I see. Then, just as this 'orrible-looking' monster moved up 'ere, you gave it a push, or shuv, did you? Like this!" There was a loud splash, followed by gurgles and struggles, and the head of Grimbart appeared above the stream again, a mass of weed and mud.

"Yes, Mr. Dass," said Brock, "that's just how it was. Only it didn't have time to step aside as I did. Are you all right?" he added anxiously.

"What the dickens are you playing at, Grimbart?" said Lady Grey. "Anyway, the thing seems to have gone now. And as it happens I wanted to see you."

Grimbart Dass made a watery sound as he hauled himself out of the water for the second time that night.

"Yes," said Lady Grey, "midsummer festival; Grey Hatch; want you to attend, of course; everyone's comin'." Grimbart Dass spat out some weed.

"It's very kind of you, of course," he began.

"Don't mention it," said Lady Grey; "glad to have you along; best festival of the year!"

Grimbart Dass scraped some mud from his face.

"Year," he said, "but I've decided that I'd better just set off ..." and then he started coughing up some water.

"Eatin'," went on Lady Grey; "wasps' nests, slugs, young rabbit or two, plenty of greens; you'll love it. See you there, then—and clean yourself up a bit before you come won't you? Bit smelly, all that mud and stuff. Come on then all of you; got to get back to the cubs; no time to waste."

"Cheerio, Grimbart!"

"Cheerio, Brocka!"

"See you at the festival."

THE midsummer festival was at an end. There had been feasting, shouting and dancing. There had been games of King of the Castle played round an old tree stump, and a lot of nosing round of a clay ball that the cubs had made to play with. The cubs, in fact had become over-excited, and Lady Grey and Betsy Blair had taken them back to Grey Hatch for a bit of a rest. Brock and Tasso, Grimbart and Blair and Brocka, lay now in a clearing and gazed up at summer stars and at bats dipping above them. They had eaten well and were enjoying the quiet, tired conversation of midsummer nights that badgers for years beyond all counting must have enjoyed at the same season on Badger Hill.

"And the men," said Tasso, "no news from them."

"No noos is good noos," said Grimbart.

"Perhaps they won't come back now," said

Blair.

"Oh, they'll be back," said Tasso.

"And when they come, we'll be 'ere to meet them," said Grimbart.

Tasso rolled over onto his stomach and looked at his old friend.

"So you're not thinking of going off on your travels again?" he said.

Grimbart rose to his feet and wandered over to dog's mercury for a few last quick mouthfuls. Still chewing, he looked hard at Brocka, who was watching him.

"Don't be silly," he said at last. "I live 'ere."

"Yes," said Tasso. "The truth is that there isn't anywhere to travel *to* nowadays. The truth is that men are men and badgers are badgers. Men have spades and dogs and guns and gas, but badgers have teeth. And men have cleverness but no understanding. Until men get some understanding, we shall just have to use our teeth whenever we must, and hope for the best."

Brocka rose to her feet and wandered over to the dog's mercury, for the sight of another badger eating was something that always made her feel hungry. She moved her pretty black and white head into the herbs and began to chew.

"I'm glad you're staying," she said to Grimbart quietly.

"And I'm glad, and all," said Grimbart, also chewing. Moths and mice fluttered and whispered among trees heavy with leaves, and long-legged and long-winged insects sucked drunkenly at the bramble flowers. Down Badger Hill in the new houses, and across the great and ancient City of Canterbury, strange grey lights flickered in the windows of houses, where men sat or dozed or thought or spoke or watched television.

"*The badger is largely a nocturnal animal,*" the televisions were squawking across the city, "*and is therefore not well known. They are quite common, yet very few people have ever seen one, although these animals may live quite close to houses, and have even been known to inhabit large parks in towns. They do little harm, and are perhaps the most uselessly persecuted of all our wild animals. They are quite intelligent and interesting creatures. Although badgers are now protected by law, each year many are killed on the roads, and by sportsmen, and by gassing setts . . ."*

As the television squawked its way through the evening, and men switched it off and made their way to bed, yawning, glancing outside perhaps at the summer stars, they might, had they been up on Badger Hill above their houses—which luckily, they weren't—have heard strange noises; the screams and whoops and barks of the midsummer party that had revived itself and was starting all over again with one of Tasso's songs as it made its way across woods and downs and through orchards and thickets. It was, in Tasso's opinion at any rate, a rather beautiful song:

> *Badgers of Badger Hill*
> *Come out when stars stand still.*
> *When the moths fly*
> *And the hunting owls cry*
> *Come the night-kings of Badger Hill.*

Tasso led the singing of this lovely lyric, and luckily therefore, could not hear what Grimbart Dass was singing, which was his own ver-

sion that he privately thought much better
than his friend's:

> *The Badgers of Badger Hill*
> *Bear nobody any ill will;*
> *But you get 'em to fight*
> *In the middle of the night*
> *And they'll cut you up, they will!*